The New Call

The New Call

RMB 817
Nannup, WA 6275
AUSTRALIA

E-mail: thenewcall@thenewcall.org
www.thenewcall.org

First published in 1996 as "The Call."

First Esoteric Publishing edition—2005

Published by Esoteric Publishing
PO Box 300249
Escondido CA 92030-0249
USA

www.esotericpublishing.com

ISBN 1-889280-31-3

Cover image courtesy of the History of Science Collections, University of Oklahoma Libraries. The original black and white image is from Camille Flammarion, 1888.

This book throws light upon key issues that are relevant today during the dawn of the Aquarian age. It presents vital information regarding the great transition that our planet is about to take and reveals how humanity may best benefit from the forthcoming unprecedented occasion.

The New Call reveals essential truths of these very special times on Earth. These truths are the property of no one person, organization or decree; they belong to humanity and they will affect all humanity. Please, therefore, share this information with anyone whom you deem may benefit from its expositions.

It is our wish that the truth of these last years of a world cycle be known by all people everywhere, so that each and every person in the world may make an informed choice with regard to the unparalleled evolutionary opportunity which is today available to all mankind.

Contents

Introduction	vii
Causes and Effects—the Birth of a New World	1
Judgement Day (The Harvest Time)	7
The Urgent Need for Preparation and Purification	15
The New and the Old	19
Inner Transformation—Personal and Planetary	23
The New World Consciousness	31
The Growing Need for Networking	35
The Rise of Cooperative Communities	39
The New Race	47
A New Way	49
The Sinister Side of the New Age	57
The Liberating Path of Service	73
Keys to Awakening	81
The Most Important Message	91
The Call to Action	97
The Final Liberation	107
Maxims for the Aquarian Age	113

Introduction

IN THESE EXTRAORDINARY TIMES people are awakening all over the world to the need for cooperation upon a rapidly changing planet. Some are joining hands in a true *esprit de corps* in order to help effect the healing and upliftment of planet Earth and of all life thereupon. A growing number amongst humanity today are seeking to assist and support one another in preparation for the imminent major planetary transformations, which shall precede the foretold dawning of a much brighter world-awareness and consequently a new and more harmonious way of life. There are many more people today consciously seeking answers to philosophical and spiritual questions than ever before during Earth's history, and their search is perfectly in accord with the evolutionary stage at which the human race has arrived and the corresponding expansion of consciousness that is presently evidencing itself all around the world.

The information disclosed in this book highlights and expounds the essential causes, purposes, and short and long-term consequences of the ongoing planetary changes. These details are hereby offered to all awakening individuals and interested persons in order that timely and important information may be shared, and the gravity of its implications recognized. Thus informed, embarkation upon a process of investigation and needed preparation for that which approaches mankind may be chosen.

There are absolutely no coincidences in an intelligently-governed universe; every effect has its cause. This book has found its way to you for definite reasons. It remains privileged, however, under the Law of Free Will as to how each person will respond—or fail to respond—to this urgent Call. In order to progress and evolve upon a free-will planet, every man has the responsibility for using his own initiative. The vital information contained in this book provides an opportunity for you to make expedient choices and to elicit the appropriate action that is necessary in light of the facts.

It should be mentioned that the compilers of this book bear no allegiance to any single religious persuasion, creed, organization or society. Occasionally throughout this treatise certain historically-established quotations or key-phrases are employed from existing faiths, and this is done for the purposes of elucidation only. No single idea belongs to any one individual or group, but originating from the inner or spiritual planes, they are a universal gift and the property of no one mind. It is recommended, therefore, that due impartiality be applied by the discerning reader to the enclosed facts and explications in order that clear perception and unadulterated comprehension may ensue.

In order to attempt to circumvent further unnecessary confusion, we wish to reveal the plain truth to humanity. The sincere seeker of truth has no interest in considering anything less than the relevant, dependable and authentic facts. In being dedicated to the truth, we do not care to allure supporters of our vision by disseminating pleasing half-truths, attractive and fashionable exaggerations or vague euphemisms that may encourage misguided zeal and excitement, or which might contribute toward misunderstanding. Esoteric knowledge may become a curse for one who is only partially informed and who may subsequently become impelled to exhibit their fragmentary learning with a hasty passion fired by self-interest. This is everywhere evidenced today as the real and important facts underlying the global transitions are being either whimsically diluted or glaringly embellished, seductively packaged and casually marketed to and by the uninitiated like so much common merchandise. This is most definitely not the way in which we seek to be of service to our human family.

Religious or spiritual idealism and hype have for ages been used to suppress or to avoid the whole truth. Ideals crystallize most rapidly, are quickly distorted thereby and may easily become a barrier, separating the idealist from reality and from the realization of a true vision of the coming age. That which is new, vital, liberating and pregnant with meaning and purpose is so ready *today* to precipitate within the consciousness of mankind and so be actively realized on Earth, but is being hindered from so doing by the idealists of the world, and far more in fact than by the ordinary person. Those eager and excitable individuals and groups around the planet, with their subjective perspectives, personal desires and neatly-formulated ideals are so often blinded by the *future* promise of glory but remain oblivious to the very real and *present* opportunities.

Most people in the world at this time respond positively only to teachers and teachings that arouse their imagination and stimulate their illusions. The unadorned truth, however, does not do this; if it did it would only present yet another impediment to real spiritual progress. This book is the result of an earnest and one-pointed endeavor to unveil the complete and unpretentious truth of that which is relevant during today's dawning Aquarian age. It does not highlight only certain selected fragments taken from the larger picture in order merely to please, to confer a false sense of security or comfort, and, therefore, to win acclaim. The elucidations herein expose both the sinister side of that which has been termed the *New Age movement* as well as its divine promise, for if true understanding is to be attained, then it must be comprehensive, and therefore all the facts must be considered side-by-side: the light *and* the dark, the good *and* the evil. However, many people demonstrate a tendency to repudiate the reality of evil in the world and, therefore, to condemn as negative any factual message that seeks to reveal the whole picture. Such a subjective attitude often gives occasion to the complete and unreasonable rejection of an important or even essential truth which, nonetheless, may appear as ominous and affronting to the brittle, reactive and unprepared mind. Yet it is only by shining a light into darkness that we are able to see clearly and so deal with the shadow side of life in a positive way. It is *understanding* that transforms us, not merely the desire for change, and until a man obtains a thorough understanding of the nature of evil and so becomes equipped to respond wisely to its challenges, he will necessarily be detrimentally affected by it. Until we truly see, acknowledge and accept what *is*, we cannot move forward from where we are; such is a basic law of life.

Truth is a correspondence with Reality, and when words of truth are heard by the open ear and perceived by the receptive heart, they elevate one's spirit and may even bring about permanent and positive transformation. In a world where fear and denial predominate, however, and where the simple truth is still regarded as an unwelcome intruder to the barricaded minds and hearts of many, the bare facts may seem like a curse. Those who choose to remain attached to their illusions are, therefore, unable to benefit from that which is true and liberating.

The impersonal truth is often resisted by the ego which, for its own security and comfort, clings to and thrives upon falsehood. Therefore, certain parts of this book are bound to prove unsettling to some. Be aware, then, that the facts detailed within these pages may appear astonishing or perhaps even entirely unbelievable and unacceptable to certain individuals; they may evoke ego-reactions as challenge, which may threaten established belief systems. But it has been said that before the eyes can see clearly, they must be free of tears; before the heart can truly understand, it must have lost its tendency to react.

This book contains indispensable keys to spiritual success during the forthcoming years. It is recommended, therefore, that careful reflection be given to the facts and principles presented, for everything that mankind needs to understand in order to be prepared for that which lies just a little way ahead for us all is contained herein.

☀ ☀ ☀

Truth is like a great rock which offers support and strength in a world of turmoil. All life yearns to know the truth, and it is the truth alone which can cure all mankind's anxieties and diseases, bestowing the peace and certitude of righteousness in exchange for unrest. All the worlds in all the universes — past, present and future — have been created so that the truth may come and make its home there. —Lord Buddha.

It is hoped that this exposition of the plain truth of the times will inform and inspire its readers to venture forth from the drudgery of typical Earthly existence in order to find the portal that leads from the old world to the New, from death to Life, and from separation and suffering to the *Final Liberation*—or Deliverance—which was promised to mankind ages ago, and which can today be realized by every sincere and intelligent person.

Causes and Effects — the Birth of a New World

TODAY, MANKIND STANDS WITNESS upon the eve of a great world transition. An unprecedented global metamorphosis is now underway which is accelerating all-round human development, bringing major changes to Earthly life and will presently lift humanity into a new era of higher awareness.

Time is measured esoterically in cycles, and on Earth the gateway to every new cycle, or age, represents a momentous milestone upon the onward journey and development of the human race. The old Piscean era has passed and all but concluded. The door leading to the next cycle: the Aquarian age, is now opening in accordance with the cosmic clockwork. As a consequence of such an epochal change, a fresh and vitalizing spirituality is dawning for humanity, bringing hitherto unknown, fundamental and positive changes to our world.

Just as planets revolve around their local sun in each solar system, so every solar system revolves around a nucleus within its galaxy and, correspondingly, each galaxy itself as a whole is in constant motion. Our own solar system is presently rotating into a new magnetic field within the galaxy, and as far as our world is concerned this movement is responsible for triggering a previously unparalleled influx of rising frequencies of cosmic energy from the inner, more subtle densities* of space. These energies are engulfing our planet at this time in accordance with a mighty Divine Plan for

---

* The term 'density' denotes a vibrational frequency of consciousness or plane of existence. The occult structure of the lower part of the universe in which we reside—the *Cosmic Physical Plane*—is most often described using a septenary model, i.e., seven ascending levels from the most dense or most material at the bottom level to the least dense or quickest vibration at the top. Each major level, or plane, can then be divided again into seven sub-levels. However, such clear-cut divisions are for conceptual convenience only, for in truth one level cannot really be distinguished from the next since the whole spectrum of vibratory frequencies changes by extremely subtle gradations. The most prevalent level of consciousness amongst the mass of human beings on Earth today, using the septenary model, is that of third-density approaching fourth.

the Earth, the solar system and beyond; they are radically affecting human consciousness and are precipitating very auspicious spiritual opportunities for mankind as a New World is about to be born.

The Earth transformation of greatest consequence will take place most swiftly and will be a tangibly objective result of that which has already transpired within the hidden worlds. The stepping up of the planetary frequency has, up to this time, been gradual and relatively subtle; its effects have even passed unnoticed to date by most people in the world. However, it is the *rending of the veil between dimensions* that is sudden, and not the developments of the preparatory stages leading up to the Great Shift; a shift which is now very close indeed.

The reader is assured that there is much truth underlying the various disseminations in the world today that pertain to the spiritual renaissance of the New Age, but the exact significance, true perspective and gravity of the times are being much distorted by the grasping minds and excited desires of mankind. There most certainly *is* a great storm approaching the Earth. This factual statement—the probable events of which were known and foretold by our prophets, saints and mystics thousands of years ago and heretofore—should be regarded as being closer to a euphemism than to an exaggeration. Like a rainstorm, one of the chief and concluding effects of the impending tempest will be that of purification, global purification.

Various purificatory symptoms of the current inflow of new energies are to be observed already in the world, and these will continue to manifest with increasing potency as the planetary vibration is progressively raised in compliance with divine order. This process of global purgation may be likened to that of a fever as it expels toxins from a sick body, and no one today can deny that the body of our planet is indeed ailing. However, for those who have prepared themselves due to their understanding of the present world crisis and opportunity, the new inflowing energies are and will continue to be responsible for many positive spiritual awakenings as they help to transmute human consciousness in readiness to receive new light. Consequently, and more than ever before, *Love* will be experienced and so given in the momentous times ahead by those who are able, and this is the goal of the transition into the age of Aquarius because since Love has ever been the harmonizing and unifying principle of Creation, it is Love alone that will heal our planet and ensure the successful building of the New World.

Today, as the expanding frequencies of Love continue to exert tension from within the inner worlds—like a new germ-seed preparing for emergence from its pod buried in the darkness of the soil in springtime—a growing pressure is inevitably being felt by mankind all around the planet. This tension gives the impression that conflict and enmity is growing in the world, that greed and iniquity are escalating. While this is certainly true in an empirical sense, everything is in order, and only an appreciation of the larger picture is able to reveal the perfection of current and impending world events. For the husk that surrounds the pregnant seed is breaking apart in order to make way for new life.

It is an immutable fact that in a dualistic universe the bright, positive and appreciably beautiful part of the Cosmos necessitates the existence of its opposite, its contrast, and this has always been and ever will be essential to the movement and development of consciousness. However, there has been an unbalanced and growing shadow looming over the Earth for millennia now, and our world has today become near-saturated by ignorance and evil. Yet such a distressing global condition was never intended for our planet, which was once known as the *Jewel of the Solar System*. The Earth is today reluctantly referred to as *the dark planet* by various benevolent entities with whom we share our universe. Fortunately, however, and by divine decree, this will presently be remedied in the Aquarian age, yet prior to the inevitable transmutation of all gross energies that constitute the plague of the Earth, the effects of untold ignorance and injustice reaching back for ages into the past must first rise up in order to be seen, addressed and healed. The whole planet is currently witnessing the darkest hour before a new dawn as the early stages of its destined and vital cleansing process unfolds.

Due to the infectious nature of the rising darkness upon Earth today, the need for rectitude and for the practice of virtue has never been so critical in the history of mankind, for *like attracts like*. Those who choose to remain inconsiderate of others and, therefore, of the Greater Life are finding that their selfish attitudes are being uncomfortably exaggerated as a result of the purging nature of the new energies. Should such individuals fail to amend their unfavorable dispositions toward life, this process will culminate for them in some kind of psychological, emotional or even physical malady. New and sometimes clinically-incurable diseases are already appearing today as symptoms of humanity's ordained and unavoidable detoxification process. Anxiety, stress, depression and a whole host of other disorders are to be observed escalating in the world, especially for those who, having little understanding of the hidden forces and purposes behind today's global transformations, tend to aggravate their own problems by reacting imprudently. For those lacking in spiritual awareness and who have become so habitually enmeshed in living solely for self that they are unwilling or unable to change, various forms of mental and emotional deterioration will continue to give rise to a pandemic of neurosis, psychosis and occult possession by discarnate entities. Conversely, however, for the selfless and large-hearted, whose lives are naturally disposed toward goodwill and love, such afflictions will be greatly minimized.

Nevertheless, however poised and detached a person may be in terms of their inner life, everyone will necessarily be influenced to some degree by prevailing world conditions, for the effects of the cumulative and harmful thought-currents and attitudes of humanity are pervasive worldwide and are sorely evident today not only in the lives of individuals but also upon the physical planet. We have generally treated the Earth with gross disrespect for far too long. We have regarded our home together with its mineral, vegetable and animal kingdoms most carelessly, and we have repeatedly demonstrated an attitude of negligence that betrays mankind's erroneous view that the resources of the planet are for its own selfish uses and exploitation alone. Humanity, as a whole, has completely overlooked the fact that Mother Earth—Gaia—is a spiritual being, engaged in her own evolutionary development, and who lovingly endeavors to provide a perfectly balanced environment for the harmonious existence of multifarious life-forms, including human beings.

The subject of impending Earth changes as a corollary of mankind's negligence and wrongdoing is a well-vented issue around the world today, and the geophysical aspects of the planetary events to come will not be detailed here. However, even though humanity has to some degree apparently understood the immediate crisis with which all life is faced upon the planet, we have clearly indicated that we are either unwilling or incapable of rectifying the extensive global damage that we ourselves have inflicted. So the pollution continues and still the rape of planet Earth and the prostitution of her resources persists. The patient intelligence of Nature will only allow such abuse to persevere up to a certain critical point, enduring mankind's violations for as long as possible in order that we may be given ample opportunity to learn from our mistakes and therefore change our ways of our own free will. Such is the great compassion of Mother Earth for her children.

In the past, the unseen Guides of the race (commonly known as the planetary or spiritual Hierarchy of Great Souls) have recognized the necessity of standing by while the forces set up by our own ignorance proceeded to react upon us, thus demonstrating the consequences of our thoughtlessness and foolish actions. In such compensating circumstances it was anticipated that we might readjust our lives appropriately and change our ways of subsistence and leisure by ceasing to ravage and to pollute the Earth, thus saving both our planet and ourselves from unnecessary and traumatic results. Therefore, humanity was given adequate occasion to discover that disengagement from selfishness, greed and materialism carries its own reward, and it was hoped that we would have liberated ourselves due to our education of suffering and hence that we would have begun to live an intelligent life in harmony with natural law.

To the contrary, however, as a race we have demonstrated our extreme failure to react positively and appropriately to the warning signs afforded us by Nature, and so today humanity and planet Earth are uncomfortably close to a red-alert condition. Symptoms of today's crisis are numerous. For example, new strains of malignant viruses are emerging in a world overladen with evil karma, for the world-ego is catharting as it has never done before. The escalating human distress is also due to a quickening of the Law of Cause and Effect upon the planet, for as the planetary vibration rises the power of thought and emotion is magnified, affecting all of life much more tangibly and swiftly than heretofore. Esotericists down the long corridors of mankind's history have always been aware that negative and self-centered thinking and emotion are responsible for all disease; it is ever thought and feeling which are the essential cause of physical-plane effects, for action always follows these.

Now, it is not the intention of this text to instill or encourage fearful reactions by presenting information that the average reader may prefer not to know about. In fact fear would only compound the aforementioned adversities. Indeed, it is world-fear that must be transmuted by love and understanding before the New World can be born. Mankind fears only that which is not understood. Fear is, therefore, a synonym for ignorance. Ignorance, in turn, is responsible for the creation of all disharmony, and thus it is ignorance that must be dissipated by the light of Truth before freedom from suffering may be known. The fearful and unintelligent denial or disregard of impending planetary developments is not helpful and will certainly not diminish them or prevent them from occurring. However, in the light of true knowledge, by the acquisition of right understanding, in the enlightened change of our thinking and attitudes, and in our consequent expedient action, the undesirable side-effects of the global purification may, by and for each individual, be alleviated and, in exceptional cases, even be transcended altogether.

To give an example of the positive advantages of an informed awareness: mainstream science has not ascertained why killer-viruses are fatal to some but not all. The reason is clear, however, to anyone who possesses elementary occult knowledge. Everything in the universe consists of energy at varying frequencies of vibration. Viruses arise due to the low and deleterious vibrations of our own negative thinking and emotion; viruses thrive at low vibratory rates. Those with an altogether higher vibration of consciousness who are positively oriented toward selflessness and love are generally immune from the so-called killer-diseases, and without the need for harmful inoculations!

'Miracle cures' have been repeatedly recorded throughout history, and all such remedies were made possible by raising the patient's vibratory rate of consciousness so that healing forces could flow unimpeded from within the ailing person himself. This has been the case whether the cure was labeled faith-healing, white magic, God's blessing or whatever else; the true reasons are always the same, and it is ever the frequency of one's consciousness that is the key to success.

The easiest and quickest way to raise the vibration of consciousness—and certainly the safest for most people—is to make contact with the Divine in oneself, and this may be done by *focusing out of and away from the personal self and upon some higher and worthy purpose*. In fact, if in aligning with universal law, mankind were to adopt and maintain such an inclusive and expanded focus, perfect healing on all levels would eventually ensue in the world, and in most cases without the need for intermediaries like doctors or drugs etc. For the majority of the planetary population this is a vitally needed education today, and it is this lesson which the impending inner and outer upheavals prior to the birth of the New World will endeavor to impart to all who attempt to continue living within the shadows of selfishness and fear.

Judgement Day (The Harvest Time)

INSUPERABLE COSMIC FORCES began the prophesied acceleration and advancement of the Divine Plan for Earth much earlier this century, but only relatively recently has this necessary process been substantially hastened. By way of its more tangible effects, therefore, it has attracted the attention of a larger percentage of the world's population, and it is these more aware persons who are responsible for introducing today's novel thought-trends, elaborate cosmologies, expanded spiritual philosophies and new healing modalities, which collectively have come to be regarded as the *New Age movement*. The ongoing changes that are currently being so avidly discussed and researched by those who belong to this movement represent a very important preliminary phase of the Divine Plan for mankind at the end of this Piscean cycle, yet they constitute only an integral part of a much larger process, the concluding stage of which, as far as humanity is presently concerned, has generally and metaphorically come to be known as *Judgement Day*. The destiny of every single soul upon Earth is inseparably linked with this momentous and now impending time of critical human choice and planetary transformation.

These culminating world events within the vast cycles and subcycles of cosmic unfoldment have occurred many times during the past and they will continue to take place whenever the dawn of a major epoch is about to break. They present, therefore, in and of themselves, nothing new, yet the great opportunity that is offered to all life which they influence is unprecedented for that cycle.

Approximately every 25,000 years the hour of Judgement Day strikes for planet Earth, and each 75,000-year period represents a major cycle which yields its own major Judgement Day. These most important occasions present great catalysts for the spiritual advancement of accomplished souls, and some aware persons have more aptly termed such a momentous period *The Harvest Time*, signifying that all those who have learned well the lessons of the physical plane will be *harvested* into, or promoted to, a higher, more expansive level of education and experience.

In the past, certain individuals have managed to harvest themselves early. These assiduous personalities have often been referred to as 'enlightened,' and techniques of self-liberation, e.g., yoga, meditation, etc., have addressed this possibility, although *sitting for enlightenment* has ever been lengthy and difficult, and only those persons possessing an indomitable will and unyielding diligence have succeeded. Today, however, at the end of this 75,000-year major cycle, and consequently due to the tremendous spiritual opportunity afforded each and every person on Earth, it is much easier for all humanity to ascend in consciousness, and groups of souls will be harvested during the birth of the New World in accordance with their ability to attune to the grace of the present period and to thereby succeed in raising the frequency of their consciousness, for the key to success at the Harvest Time is *vibration*. Each individual's consciousness (which is an integral part of the planetary vibration) must be raised to a minimal level in order to qualify for graduation into the New World.

There are many legends of a 'Day of Judgement' at which time the future destiny of mankind is decided. Behind these legends there lies an important truth, although the fanciful imagination of certain religious adherents has in the past misinterpreted the perfectly simple and logical fact of necessary karmic reconciliation into a distorted and whimsical idea of 'everlasting damnation.' It is a perfect part of the Divine Plan that cosmic forces bring to an end cycles, ideologies, societies and civilizations when the due and right time comes. This is done in order to make place for that which is better and which will prove adequate, and not limiting, to the awakening consciousness and to the emerging life.

The Judgement Day as found in scriptural behests is a conveniently recallable simile for a necessary separation of souls, when human beings who are not sufficiently advanced to progress with the rest will be excluded from the ongoing stream of life. With regard to the imminent Judgement Day, divine ordinance will ensure that the development of such immature souls will continue upon another planet where conditions are better suited to their specific needs and more befitting to their level of evolvement.

Leading up to the 'Day of Reckoning' when the Book of Records will be opened for everyone to see, all those who have failed to take full advantage of the spiritual opportunities afforded them during many lifetimes will depart from the rounds of Earthly incarnation where a more advanced life-expression is about to begin. However, this does not mean extinction or eternal damnation of the soul, even though it does impose a considerable though incalculable delay to its onward journey. While such delay is unquestionably serious, nevertheless the universal Law of Recompense knows no biased leniency and so can show no special sympathy for those who do not *make the grade*. Such underdeveloped souls are clearly in need of more experience upon the battlefield of physical-plane life, and that experience they will be given by law, even though it may mean innumerably additional lifetimes, many of which will include much suffering. Conversely, all those souls who successfully meet the greater requirements of the impending Harvest Time will be liberated from the *wheel of rebirth* and will be entirely free of the obligation to incarnate in any of the fallen worlds on any planet ever again.

It may be recognized, then, that with regard to today's cyclic spiritual opportunity there are three distinct groups:

i. Those who, having failed to learn the lessons of the physical plane over many lifetimes, will be forced to leave the Earth in order to later incarnate on another physical world so that they may begin again to learn by way of the unique experiences and opportunities that are available only in the third density.

ii. Those who have learned sufficiently from and passed the tests of the physical-plane school and who will have therefore earned their promotion to the fourth- or fifth-density classroom of life where they shall proceed with their higher learning. It should be understood that such a graduation does not mean Liberation or perfect Enlightenment, and the promoted soul will at some stage in the future be compelled by karmic law to return, via reincarnation, to the physical plane in order to once again attempt to achieve the one Goal of every unenlightened human being: *transfiguration*, or ultimate Liberation from matter (including the more subtle matter of the fourth and fifth densities). Therefore, the graduation to the fourth or fifth densities is actually a temporary promotion into more rarefied spheres of existence and experience, and so may be termed 'the lesser harvest.'

iii. Those who have discovered and gone the Path of Return[*] and who are, therefore, able to be lifted up into the sixth cosmic

---

[*] The Path of Return and its requirements—scarcely known but vital esoteric information—is available to all earnest and intelligent seekers (see end of book).

sphere—the *Body of Christ*—and so who will attain the Final Liberation from all the lower worlds of fallen nature by being harvested back into the divine Kingdom. This is the true Harvest and has been the prime focus of all Avatars throughout human history.

* * *

Most Christians today do not fully realize that a vital part of the great mission of Jesus two thousand years ago was to attempt to prepare humanity for this present time of unprecedented planetary transformation and spiritual opportunity. It was with the objective of saving as many souls as possible from avoidable delay and suffering that the Piscean Christ said to his disciples: *"Go ye into all the world and preach the gospel to every creature; he that believeth and is baptized shall be saved, but he that believeth not shall be damned."* For baptism, and its corresponding rites in other religions, is a sign of the dedication of one's life in service to the Divine Plan and to humanity, and the one who grasps the truth of universal law and so resolutely forgets the self in order to look forward and upward in the right direction, will certainly be amongst the *saved* who escape the "damnation" of the succeeding Judgement Day. The word "damned" is indicative of the rejection from the present life-current which is about to be promoted, and a throwing back into the preceding of the successive life-streams; a veritable damnation indeed for all those who would prefer to move ahead spiritually and to behold the splendor of a new human consciousness and a new world.

After the Great Separation—the period of which Jesus referred to as "The Sifting Time," what the Koran terms "Kiyamat," and which immediately precedes the new era that the Mayan Prophecy calls "The Golden Age"—world conditions will be specially adapted for the rapid progress of the more advanced souls, and will therefore be wholly unsuitable for those who are at a much lower stage of development. The more intense frequencies of energy upon the planet in the future would not rouse the higher nature of the less-developed man, but would instead stimulate and amplify his lower passions, so that while he would not himself benefit by being on Earth at that time, he would also present difficulties for the progress of the more advanced souls. The New World stands ready and waiting today to admit humanity into its higher vibratory field of life, but those who have failed to learn the vital lessons which it has been their choice to learn or not to learn for many incarnations, will be unable to venture forth due to incompatibility of vibration; such is a fundamental ruling decreed by the forthcoming Judgement Day.

✷ ✷ ✷

The Sheep and the Goats
From The Aquarian Gospel of Jesus the Christ

33 Be ready at every moment of the day and night, because when you expect him not the Lord will come.

34 Behold, when he will come with all his messengers of light, the Book of Life, and that of Records, shall be opened up — the books in which the thoughts and words and deeds are written down.

35 And everyone can read the records he has written for himself, and he will know his doom before the judge shall speak, and this will be the sifting time.

36 According to their records men will find their own.

37 The judge is Righteousness, the king of all the Earth, and he will separate the multitudes as shepherds separate the sheep and goats.

38 The sheep will find their places on the right, the goats upon the left, and every man will know his place.

39 And then the judge will say to those upon the right, "You blessed of the Father-God, come unto your inheritance, which was prepared for you from times of old.

40 "You have been servants of the race; I was hungry and you gave me bread; was thirsty and you gave me drink; was naked and you gave me clothes;

41 *"Was sick, you ministered to me; was in prison and you came to me with words of cheer; I was a stranger and in your homes I found a home."*

42 *Then will the righteous say, "When did we see you hungry, thirsty, sick, imprisoned or a stranger at our gates and ministered to you?"*

43 *And the judge will say, "You served the sons of men, and whatsoever you have done for these, that you have done for me."*

44 *The judge will say to those upon the left, "Depart from me; you have not served the sons of men.*

45 *"I was hungry and you gave me naught to eat; was thirsty and you gave me naught to drink; was a stranger and you drove me from your door; I was imprisoned and was sick, you did not minister to me."*

46 *Then these will say, "When did we thus neglect to care for you? When did we see you hungry, thirsty, sick, a stranger or in prison and did not minister to you?"*

47 *And then the judge will say, "Your life was full of self; you served the self and not your fellow man, and when you slighted one of these, you slighted and neglected me."*

48 *Then will the righteous have the kingdom and the power, and they who are unrighteous shall go forth to pay their debts, to suffer all that men have suffered at their hands.*

49 *They who have ears to hear and hearts to understand will comprehend these parables.*

* * *

Past examples of Harvest Times can be verified by referring to esoteric history. The great catastrophe that destroyed Atlantis many thousands of years ago was a veritable Judgement Day of a similar yet lesser order to that which is now impending, and which will, as it did in the end times of Atlantis, reject all those souls who are unqualified to proceed with the remainder of the race. It is probable that in Atlantean times, just as in our own, many or even most people failed to believe or heed the warning signs, their prophets or their predictions, yet today a little intelligent observation and research will highlight clearly to those who remain objective what shall be.

It is plainly evident to all of discerning awareness that, owing to their materialistic attitudes, those who cling to the old and outmoded ways of life will be unfit to continue side by side with the more spiritually-oriented population in the New World. Therefore, it may be seen just how critical it is in these times to subscribe sincerely and fully to all that is new, relevant and righteous, for the Harvest Time is at hand. A mere interest in the truth of the times is most definitely not sufficient. Cursory inquisitiveness never managed to raise anyone's vibration by very much and will certainly not, by itself, produce a positive result at the Harvest Time. It is the *demonstration of love* alone that shall positively affect a person's consciousness. Therefore, active and altruistic response to the present need is demanded today in order for success to be known, not passive acquiescence.

The Urgent Need for Preparation and Purification

IF WE COULD LOOK DOWN from outer space upon the earth with clairvoyant vision we would see the psycho-emotional aura of the planet as a murky ball of seething mist, steam and fog. We might stand aghast at beholding this great dark cloud of subtle matter, which would evidence itself to be of a density and thickness that indicated not only impenetrability but also those conditions that are unfavorable to life and which make all things appear unclear and distorted. Thus it would be appreciated that there is a pressing need for change and global decontamination, for preparation by all those upon Earth who would be ready to weather well the approaching purificatory storm and, moreover, who would be advantaged by it.

Tribulation will be experienced globally during the coming years, and effort spent solely in sympathetically administering to emotional or mental suffering and in applying temporary remedies to the growing external symptoms of a world ailing from an internal, spiritual sickness, is not perhaps the most expedient exercise of one's labor in these exceptional times. Patching up the multiplying wounds of humanity, while being both a necessary and noble duty, is becoming an extremely daunting task for humanitarians today, and soon enough there will not be a sufficient supply of *band-aids* to go around, or indeed nurses to apply them!

Due to the tangible results of their ministrations, many healers today may fancy that they accomplish a complete service. However, in the majority of cases and upon closer scrutiny such a view may be seen to be erroneous. Once relieved of the *symptoms* of their ailment—be they physical, emotional or mental—most people tend to become quite satisfied; they often revert back to their routine pattern of living and so fail to begin a search for the underlying *causes* of their illness. If discovered and understood, however, the essential reasons for their trouble would indicate an appropriate new direction in life for them to take in order that they may move forward while simultaneously effecting a permanent remedy for themselves.

The majority of individuals today seek healing for themselves alone, i.e., with selfish motives. Such personal objectives will not serve to raise their vibratory rate of consciousness; indeed, to the contrary. It may be that certain curative applications do free patients so that their spiritual seeking and service can then proceed unimpeded. However, should a greater understanding of the essential causes of disease fail to be elicited in addition to personal relief, then in light of that which presently looms upon mankind's horizon and when regarded spiritually, such treatment is without lasting value. Should the complete solution be absent from healing services, if the root-cause is left unaddressed and re-education neglected, then temporarily-cured symptoms of illness will only reappear in one form or another, for true healing must necessarily include right understanding.

The purpose of disease is not merely to provide humanity with an opportunity to discover how to eradicate it! Disease is an effect of a corresponding cause. It therefore bears within itself an important *lesson* for its creator, a lesson that cannot be learned as long as one's attitude toward the self-created disease is antagonistic, as long as one wishes only to stamp it out. However, in remedying the cause of the problem by *learning the lesson*, the effects of disease will eventually disappear by themselves, never to return. Such is true and permanent healing.

The proliferation of new healing techniques today during the birth of the Aquarian age, in encouraging a focus upon *self* as they generally do, often serve to feed the fires of desire in the patient and pride in the healer, thereby diverting many from the real and serious issues with regard to the present period. True and permanent healing is inner, spiritual healing, of which humanity is most desperately in need, along with the preventive medicine of contemporarily-relevant education. Such befitting measures will contribute significantly toward the vitally-required change, preparation and purification of a race which has ventured distressingly close today to self-destruction due to its prevailing ignorance.

Practical discernment is urgently needed at this critical hour, a discernment that will lead to *healing through helpfulness*. Generally, the greatest good that anyone can confer at this time upon Earth—for others as well as for themselves—is to help toward raising the planetary vibration, and this may be achieved by truly benevolent thinking and selfless, loving activity. As a healer expands his awareness to embrace the greater purposes and laws of life, his desire to see tangible results in the material world will begin to fall away as he becomes conscious of the deeper levels to which his healing ministrations penetrate. True, spiritual understanding will enable such a person to appreciate his contribution toward the more important needs of the soul, and therefore the causal levels of the human psyche, without placing undue importance upon immediate or physical results. Love is the greatest healer, of course, although its effects may sometimes not be instantly recognizable on the physical plane.

The most potent catalyst for education, purification, comprehensive healing and spiritual progress in these times preceding the birth of the New World is to be found in positive and purposeful human interactions, for under the Law of Relationship, life presents its lessons most expeditiously. Indeed, relationship is the mirror in which we discover ourselves. However, due to the intensity of the period we would all do well to make an earnest endeavor to swiftly heal any unhealthy or unbalanced associations, or remove ourselves from them where such healing is impossible, for all attachments and tensions within relationships will cause progressively more distress in the rapidly changing times ahead. Depending upon the purity of one's motives and orientation toward helpfulness, rests the possibility of utilizing today's spiritual opportunities successfully; the grace of the Aquarian age may best be attracted in meaningful and loving relationship with others.

> *Every one to whom I speak has in him all the fires of God; but they are lying dead. The will is bridled by desires of the flesh, and it brings not the ethers of the fires to vibrate into light. Look, therefore, to your soul and note, is not the light within you dark as night? There is no breath but Holy Breath that e'er can fan your fires of life into a living flame and make them light. And Holy Breath can raise the ethers of the fires to light in none but hearts of purity and love. Hear, then, make pure the heart, admit the Holy Breath, and then your bodies will be full of light, and like a city on a hill, your light will shine afar, and thus your light may light the way for other men.*—Jesus.

Purify and Prepare! is the urgent cry of the New Spirit heard everywhere today by those with ears to hear. The impending and necessary cleansing of the Earth and of all sentient life thereupon may be difficult or moderate for each individual depending upon the degree of preparation attained. Efforts made and time spent upon the urgent process of purification—the most vital aspects being psychological and emotional—is now crucial faced with what lies ahead. It is extremely important to begin to effect the required preparations immediately so that a smooth and positive transition may ensue. Effective and lasting purification begins with right understanding. Anyone who remains unacquainted with the nature of that which is transpiring today is at an extreme disadvantage and will become progressively more handicapped during the approaching years as the incoming streams of Aquarian energy intensify. Today all is moving, changing, becoming. This fact must be seen and addressed in order that a true recognition may be gained regarding the present world-transformations, together with a lucid perception, acknowledgment and intelligent acceptance of the ever-widening rift between that which is new and that which is now swiftly becoming obsolete.

The New and the Old

ALL THAT IS OF THE NEW—philosophy, religion, science, spirituality, etc.—is today revealing itself in conspicuous contrast to the old and outworn standards as a major division develops on a grand scale. Unremittingly the split between the two yawns steadily wider and is now beginning to evidence itself prominently in the physical world. Such a division is apparent to those who are aware and who therefore consciously recognize the current indications of what must ultimately transpire. The mass-media, however, cannot be relied upon to impart the truth of the times for it is not good for business!, and the serious investigator will need to look elsewhere. *"Seek and ye shall find; knock and the door will be opened."* Today's earnest and thoroughgoing enquirer will soon discover that immense changes have commenced their inevitable unfoldment upon Earth, and that we are living in very unique times.

The gravity of the period and the magnitude of its impending major effects cannot be easily overstated. There exist numerous references in many and diverse texts, including established scriptures, that suggest the days of what Christianity terms 'Armageddon' are near at hand. Secular and scientific minds are also making intelligent inference, based upon modern research and contemporary trends, as to what is occurring in our solar system and, therefore, what may ensue globally as a result. For example, unusual planetary configurations are expected in the time leading up to the second decade of the twenty-first century, and much evidence has been examined by our scientists which indicates that a shift of the planet's poles is probable at some time during that period.[*] A plethora of other prophecies and geological predictions currently abound, and it is partly due to such grave forecasts as well as the present, tangible physical-plane symptoms of today's world-transformation that a greater appreciation of the interconnectivity of everything within Creation is emerging amidst humanity.

New and higher levels of perception are dawning for many people in the world, as previously hidden realities are being revealed to those who are receptive. Psychism is in much greater proliferation amongst the general populace today than has ever

---

[*] It is known that such great shifts of the Earth's axes have occurred many times before throughout the ages.

been known before, and many sensitives are beginning to benefit from the guiding Law of Synchronicity and other miscellaneous occult phenomena, which are now manifesting spontaneously in their lives.

As a new world-ethic emerges in the awareness of awakening humanity, more and more individuals are seeing that separation on any level is destructive; a relic of ignorance from the past, and that cooperation and unity are the goals and indeed the prerequisites of the immediate future. Antagonism and fear are at last being recognized as harmful to all life, while active goodwill is seen as the touchstone that will transform the world.

The Aquarian transition is today well underway, and as new life-energies flood the planet, animating world awareness and so coercing change, every human being is faced with a vitally important choice. Whether they wish to or not, whether they understand or not, each and every person is today being compelled to make a choice that shall greatly affect both the present course of their lives and their future soul-development, throughout incalculable incarnations. It must be emphasized that this choice will be determined by each individual's *demonstration* of his decision. It will be his ability to express and, therefore, evidence his choice that shall affect the vibratory rate of consciousness, and it is this which shall establish whether that person has opted to move forward with that which is new and vital, or whether he has chosen to stay with the old and redundant ways of being.

* * *

Now, there exist in the world separative and destructive forces that humanity has itself created or attracted in its ignorance of universal law. These are the forces of the lower self, and since their collective influence in the world is a most detrimental one they are regarded by many people as evil forces. Due to the rapidly expanding light of the emerging new paradigms for Earth, these forces already belong to the old world, and their tyrannical reign upon the planet is finally about to end. Under the laws of the Aquarian age all that is of the old is now falling into decay and will eventually dissolve completely in order to be replaced by the New. Those who remain within the relationships and thought-patterns of the old world consciousness will attract the old, degenerating energies into their lives, thereby disqualifying themselves from entering the New World.

One of the most significant maxims for this transition time warns us that whoever is in conflict with anything through resistance, worry, fear, aversion, dependence or selfish desire of it is automatically of the old to the same degree as that conflict. All those who do not recognize the need for or who fail to realize a truly spiritual and, therefore, selfless attitude will know progressively greater struggle and discord in the critical times ahead, as rising waves of new energy sweep our planet. As the Earth makes its forthcoming and prophesied leap in consciousness, we may either gracefully surf these incoming waves of opportunity or be overwhelmed by them. If the materialists of the world continue to weave their habitually exclusive and selfish designs throughout their lives, they are bound to witness the effects of the purifying energies of the Aquarian age as terribly destructive, for the imminent world changes are set to eliminate those things which they value most.

As the planetary vibration rises and as new, subtle yet potent forces pour into the invisible planes corresponding to our physical planet, a new order of life is emerging, together with the birth of a New World Consciousness. Outmoded ways of the past are and will continue to rapidly prove themselves unworthy of the new realities and thus they will nullify themselves through a process of atrophy that will eventuate in their complete and permanent eradication from planet Earth. We are living in a period of radical purification and a parting of souls. The gates of both heaven and hell are now opening wide, and every single person in the world must now make a choice one way or the other, for no one can serve two masters.

A critical time of decision has arrived for everyone. The present opportunity is so great and the need for definite and positive action is so demanding that, whether we like it or not, we are all faced with a challenge. We are confronted with one of two vital choices: either to embrace the new way of being and its intrinsic responsibilities, or to reject them in the bold acknowledgement that we are not concerned or that we are unable or unprepared to make the needed changes and sacrifices in our lives. In the very near future, one way or another, each individual will have made a necessary choice to affiliate with either the *Islands of Light* or the *caverns of darkness*; there will be no grey areas. Therefore, each member of the human family must today choose between love and fear, wisdom and ignorance. Whatever we decide in this matter will definitely affect the remainder of our days here on Earth, for we shall either throw what weight or aid we can into the One Divine Work of planetary redemption, and so prepare wisely for what is to come, or we shall join the ranks of those who regard the whole proposition as uninteresting, unbelievable, too demanding or unworthy of their time and effort. It is this second group who work subconsciously or overtly, unwittingly or deliberately, to delay what must inevitably come to pass.

The new world-paradigm necessarily possesses a dynamic expulsive power and is therefore the natural adversary of the old and obsolete, and to this fact a growing number of forward-looking individuals bear testimony. Yet the old cannot withstand the New, for such is the Divine Plan for planet Earth. Correspondingly, *the degenerative forces of the old do not have the power to affect anyone who attunes to the New.* Thus, each person today has both the marvelous opportunity and spiritual responsibility for raising their consciousness as they can in these *"end times"* by aligning themselves with the superseding paradigms.

The law is set. All those who are able to genuinely express unconditional love during the birth of the Aquarian age will automatically attune to that which is bright and new. It is thus that they shall witness all their past limitations and conflicts dissolving away as spiritual contact is established, as clarity of vision and purpose is restored in their lives, and as they rise up with a song of gratitude and joy to greet the unprecedented light of a New Day.

Inner Transformation—Personal and Planetary

WORLD CONSCIOUSNESS HAS TO DATE been predominantly governed by emotion and desire. The important lessons that are today being conveyed to humanity by the unavoidable disintegration of the old standards highlight clearly that there can be no peace or happiness without wisdom, and where there exists blind sentiment and craving, wisdom is necessarily absent. No society that is possessed by selfish desire can ever escape its own self-created sorrow and eventual ruin. This has been repeatedly illustrated throughout history by the inevitable fall of even great civilizations such as those of Rome, Greece and Constantinople. No society has ever been or will ever be exempt from universal law, and so it is today for the global society of planet Earth in this time of major transformation.

Since time immemorial there has existed an unhealthy and pervasive habit amongst humanity whereby its thoughts and attitudes have been unduly influenced, even determined, by custom, by its peers, and by 'authority.' Rather than thinking autonomously and creatively as a race, we have generally been disposed to mental passivity, to run with the pack, and this has led to a willingness to accept—or at the very least to subconsciously yield to—the common and spiritually unprogressive thought-trends of our social regime. The recognition of these facts together with their undesirable cultural ramifications is fortunately now being made by a growing number of people in the world today and is responsible for one very important shift in human thinking, namely the widespread search for meaning and a truer understanding of life. The acquisition of such understanding is enabling the intelligent members of humanity to transcend blind intensity of feeling (and the heedless thinking and action that always follow ungoverned emotion), and to sublimate it with reason and greater awareness, which will, in turn, contribute toward creating a better world.

One of the general inner transformations for mankind, then, and one that is currently being demonstrated by those who indicate potential for entry into the New World, is a shift from a predominantly emotional bias to a more mental disposition. This means that one becomes principally a thinking person who lives by the discriminating regulation of thought, feeling and action, and by expedient choices that are ever facilitated by due reflection, guided by right understanding, and are therefore ethically and sanely motivated with due regard for the whole. This is an essential part of the present transition because the Aquarian age for Earth will be the age of reason and spiritual understanding.

There are also other transformations of a more immediate and tangible nature that are being experienced around the world today. As humanity is rapidly changing on various levels simultaneously in accord with the period and the Divine Plan for Earth, people are becoming increasingly sensitive to their environment. As planetary frequencies are amplified, magnifying sensitivity as well as both favorable and adverse vibrations around the world, a growing number of people are discovering that they are much more responsive to, and therefore affected by, surrounding inner and outer mental and emotional conditions (i.e., subtle energies). Consequently, negative psycho-emotive states, e.g., anxiety, stress, worry, etc. are producing far greater palpable effects than heretofore, thereby disturbing the balance of organic processes within the body and so contributing more dramatically toward debilitation, degeneration and disease. However, this need not be so, for every person today has a choice with regard to their own immediate destiny.

The acquisition of an inclusive view of the world—whereby identification is made with all life as being an inseparable extension of oneself—will enable each individual to truly appreciate their position and responsibility as world citizens, and such a wholesome attitude will allow them to receive the new and vital energies that are flooding the planet. By attracting those energies that are intrinsically protective, life-giving and spiritualizing, the person who has chosen to set their face in the right direction will be greatly assisted in circumventing the potentially devastating phenomena that will precipitate throughout the birth of the New World, while simultaneously they will be contributing toward the successful promotion and integration of the ongoing positive changes.

It is becoming increasingly appreciated worldwide that there is an essential need for an adequate understanding of the present crisis with which mankind is faced and the implementation of necessary life-adjustments in accord with that understanding. It is being more widely recognized that only by constructive and benign thinking may we heal ourselves by rising above the dense and debilitating thought-clouds that we have unwittingly cultivated during an inimical past. That great psycho-emotional smog—perpetually fed by the ignorance, selfishness and negativity of mankind—is responsible worldwide for excessive disease and unnaturally short life spans,* and such a disharmonious psychic environment greatly hinders the well-being and natural evolution of all life that struggles under its unwholesome influence.

This overwhelming fog of subtle matter hangs oppressively over our planet today like a burial shroud, stifling, subduing and crushing the human spirit. We must swiftly alter our tendencies for spiritual suicide; we must emerge today from the ominous global shadow that we have fostered for so long; we must recognize clearly that which we are guilty of collectively perpetrating upon the Jewel of the Solar System in order to motivate the effective remedy of the cumulative damage rendered by our planetary exploitations. We must change our ways, or be devastated by the very real and direful consequences initiated by them.

It is simply not enough to be merely informed about the Aquarian age transitions. Today's exigency demands the active transmutation of the old, noxious and unacceptable energies by the intelligently-focused creation of new, benign and vital thought-currents. Thinking has for ages been the most potent faculty available to mankind. It possesses equally the power to create or to destroy. It is a far-reaching fact that all suffering is due to disharmonious thinking, while all joy, peace and harmony is born from thoughts that are in alignment with universal law.

The controlled imagination is a powerful creative force, for every thought to which we give birth becomes a living, semi-intelligent entity (sometimes called an *elemental*) upon the other side of the veil between the third density and the next, influencing humanity for good or for ill. All of the activities that we might call evil, whether unholy thoughts or negative emotions, invariably manifest themselves as vibrations in the more coarse matter upon subtle planes, whilst good and unselfish thought or emotion sets in vibration the higher types of matter. As finer matter is much more

---

* A clean psychic atmosphere would enable mankind to realize an average longevity of perhaps 500 years or more together with a corresponding improvement in the quality of that life. Incredible life spans of 700+ years are documented in ancient scripts, and these refer to a time when the planet was much healthier.

readily stirred into responsive activity than is coarse, it follows that a given amount of force spent in good thought or feeling produces a result that is many times greater than the same amount of force projected into coarser matter. In terms of value and lasting positive effect, just one unselfish and loving thought may contain the potency of a hundred negative thoughts.

It will be especially advantageous in the years ahead for everyone to understand well that if there is in the human aura no matter (vibration) capable of response, then negative thought-currents cannot permanently affect that person at all. A pure heart and mind are the best protection against inimical assaults of thought and feeling. However, mankind may take one step beyond mere self-protection, for the vibration of Love is both the greatest protector *and* benefactor in the whole universe. With spiritual understanding, therefore, humanity may begin to use its natural capacity to generate thought-force for the benefit and upliftment of all life.

In reviewing esoteric history we may discover that past civilizations elsewhere in the Cosmos managed to completely annihilate themselves together with their whole planet, and this was due to the inevitable outcome that ensues when a world becomes entirely saturated with negativity. However, Mother Earth is not going to implode and disintegrate just yet! Indeed, this will never be allowed to happen, for as a vital organ in the Solar Body, and also as a nexus of indispensable knowledge and information, our planet is far too important to many other forms of life throughout our galaxy. Essential data is encoded within the mineral, vegetable, animal and human kingdoms upon Earth, and it is partly in order to access this information that humanity is witnessing today an escalating frequency of extraterrestrial visitations, abductions and general alien interference and experimentation upon the planet. Furthermore, as mankind has clearly demonstrated that it is incapable of saving the world or itself, other more advanced beings from multifarious origins are intervening in our destructive course, for the Earth must be healed and redeemed before the New World can be born.

Armageddon is nigh, but it is not the end of the world for humanity as some people have misconstrued; to the contrary, it is the birth of a new beginning. Specifically, the word 'Armageddon' means *a final and conclusive battle between the forces of good and evil*; an entirely befitting description indeed for our times. Our planet has eons of development yet to experience throughout the far distant future, and so to ensure that unfavorable circumstances do not evolve beyond the point of no return (which they certainly would if mankind was left to its own devices!), the Forces of Light, which always prevail over darkness and ignorance, have been entering the subtle spheres corresponding to our planet for some time now in order to purify and restore balance and peace here again. Humanity is soon to return to a relative *Garden of Eden*, which the Earth once was, but which was lost due to mankind's ignorance and unwise use of free will; our misguided choosing of greed and selfishness instead of charity and love.

Returning to the present now, it is most apparent that there is much discord and tension predominating generally in the world today. As was indicated previously, our environs inevitably affect our consciousness, and this is so particularly for those who are sensitive. As tension rises within the mind and emotions of a man, his subtle energy fields become inflamed and so are much more likely to impinge detrimentally upon the auras and, therefore, the consciousness of others around him. Auric contamination is especially intensified in cities and other highly populated areas for obvious reasons. Additionally, as sensitivity is heightened for all humanity in accord with the ongoing changes, toxic emanations such as electromagnetic frequencies (EMF), air and noise pollution, and unnatural and noxious substances like chemical additives in foods, etc., are causing greater adversity for the reactive majority.

A fundamental understanding of the inner constitution of man will be extremely helpful in accepting and living optimistically amidst the inevitable transformations that are already today affecting everyone on various levels. The etheric (subtle energy) body, that partly constitutes the human aura, is a receiver (and transmitter) of vibrational forces and energies, and is inseparably linked to its etheric *chakras* (energy centers) through which flow the new Aquarian frequencies from the higher planes. Each chakra, in turn, is directly associated with an endocrine gland and certain nerve plexuses in the physical body. Due to their close relationship with the chakras, the endocrine and nervous systems of mankind are today undergoing radical changes: a process of transmutation. The intensification of subtle energies upon Earth, both externally and from within, necessitates a complete *rewiring* of the physical and subtle nervous systems. Additionally, the organs and glands in the physical body are being upgraded in order that they too may sustain the increased frequencies that are steadily streaming into the planet in preparation for the Great Shift. Humanity, then, is being reorganized upon cellular, atomic, subatomic and ethereal levels.

Within the human vehicles of consciousness (which include many layers of subtle energy in the aura), there exists a great storehouse of biological data which is being stimulated and released by today's higher frequencies. The new energies are also activating previously dormant areas of the brain (including the pineal and pituitary glands) as they are simultaneously affecting the chromosomes and DNA/RNA in each cell, consequently opening up latent intuitive faculties and activating miscellaneous subtle stimuli which are eliciting psychic awakenings in many.

Certain levels of the human constitution will be affected more than others at different times as the planetary shifts ensue. Many observable symptoms of the ongoing changes are transpiring today for humanity, and these include: anxiety, irritability, tension, nervousness, restlessness, depression, confusion, worry, fear, forgetfulness, insomnia, visionary experiences, various changes in awareness, lucid-dreaming, unexpected and often uncontrollable catharsis, e.g., sorrow, laughter, exhilaration, etc. Physical symptoms may include: headaches, muscle soreness, joint pains, disruptive digestion, loss of appetite, fatigue, stomach-ache, heart palpitations, muscle spasms, allergies, etc. Sometimes the human vehicles will expend energy at irregular rates, oscillating between hyperactivity and unusual sluggishness. At times the physical body may require certain nutrients in quantities that it did not need previously, and many people today are feeling a demand to change their diet to lighter, unrefined, raw and more vital foodstuffs.

Positive thoughts and healthy emotions react most favorably upon both the subtle and physical bodies of man and improve their ability to assimilate life-force and to receive other beneficial energies. The endocrine system is responsible for secreting hormones and other substances into the bloodstream, and such natural activity is increased in response to emotional reactions to life experience; an experience which is today growing more intense for everyone. Our inner biological pharmacopoeia is triggered in accordance with the unique events passed through and the subsequent choices made by each individual. For example, anger releases adrenalin, while elation releases endorphins. As new energies are received, translated by each person's awareness and consequently expressed in a unique way, one's positive or negative responses will determine subtle and physical reactions that shall precipitate the corresponding beneficial or detrimental effects upon all levels of one's constitution.

INNER TRANSFORMATION—PERSONAL AND PLANETARY 29

As the physical, etheric, emotional, mental and higher vehicles of consciousness are all interconnected, an effect in any one of them will generally influence the others to some degree. Favorable chemical release will serve to catalyze higher vibratory rates in the human vehicles and so assist with the transition into a more elevated and expanded awareness. It may be helpful to compare the aforementioned effects with those of psychoactive drugs, which function in the same way and may consequently induce similar but temporary results in consciousness. However, the effects elicited by the waves of energy during the birth of the New World will be naturally induced and permanent.

Negative reactions to symptoms of purification, i.e., antagonistic thoughts and emotions, will result in the introduction of toxins into the bloodstream, and in causing chemical imbalances these will, of course, hinder the important process of positive transformation. The secretion and circulation of poisons in the physical body will effect a corresponding lowering of vibration in the vehicles of consciousness, and this will contribute significantly toward an increased susceptibility to adverse environmental influences of all kinds, for like attracts like. In order to be received, the inflowing Aquarian energies demand humble, open and surrendered channels. Humanity must therefore be informed and aware at this time in order that prudent choices may be made in response to global processes rather than unwitting reactions.

Clearly, then, there may be one of two possible responses of consequence to the influx of the new energies:

1. Those who choose, with awareness, discrimination and trust, to attune to the higher energies will experience purification, transmutation, expeditious inner growth, positive expansions of consciousness and spiritual unfoldment as they are aided by the rising Aquarian frequencies and as they are catalyzed into awakening. Such discerning persons will behold their consciousness rising naturally to new heights of experience and expression, and they will enjoy the greatest freedom and capacity for love that they have ever known in their lives. Eventually, together with the discovery of a marvelous new agility and vitality born within their finely-tuned bodies, they will open up to a much greater flow of spiritual energy via their refined nervous systems, and they will finally graduate most joyfully during the impending Harvest Time.

2. Those who are unwilling or unable to release old and deleterious character-patterns shall witness an unpleasant accumulation of blocked energy in their bodies, and this may culminate in the gross magnification of previously-tempered or suppressed personality traits, these latter being discharged with increasingly uncontrolled furor to the detriment of themselves and others around them.

The human dense and subtle energy systems are inseparably linked to those of the Earth. Therefore, as humanity is purified and transformed, our whole globe is concurrently and similarly affected, and vice-versa. The planetary energy grid (the Earth's nervous system) and its vortex network (the chakra system of the planet) are today undergoing a process of fundamental change. Some old vortexes are atrophying and dying, whilst others are being vivified, and even new vortexes are appearing, all in accord with the Divine Plan for our planet, which shall ensure the successful emergence of the New World Consciousness for planet Earth.

The New World Consciousness

THE AQUARIAN AGE BRINGS WITH IT new and adjusted laws for the advanced progress of mankind in various fields, and these laws are perfectly suited to the expanding world-consciousness today. As the whole planet moves onto its next and highest turn of the evolutionary spiral, humanity is being exhorted by the new laws and by the divine Agents who implement them, to realize unity and true spiritual fellowship: a new and harmonious way of being. Such an ideal is not only possible in this concluding period of the Piscean era, but is also a prerequisite for the redemption and healing of both the Earth and mankind.

Many of the old ways of religious thinking and living have proven to create more problems than solutions, and those individuals who will aid in the emergence of the New World Consciousness are now readily relinquishing the old methods altogether and are turning wholeheartedly toward the new presentations of truth. A great change of attitude is underway throughout the world and it is being recognized, particularly in the West, that the old ways of self-oriented spiritual advancement no longer apply as they once did, and that the search for personal enlightenment cannot be a part of the new world-ethic. In the new era selfish spiritual ambition will be entirely superseded by earnest dedication to the collective good. Those who are awakening today to the need for change have learned from the old ways and they are ready to surrender them for something much more currently significant, vital, opportune and expansive. Intelligent humanity is now ready to transcend blind faith and the need for external objects of worship, religious intermediaries, techniques of self-liberation and complex philosophical ideals. These methods are simply no longer serving the present spiritual needs of mankind. A growing number of aware and thinking people in the world today are recognizing that personality must give way to impersonality, self must yield to Spirit if peace is ever to reign upon Earth, and it is these awakening individuals who comprise the *critical mass* which shall enable the New World Consciousness to be born and to become permanently established.

In order that the new world-paradigm of a united awareness may become a reality, ideas originating from the spiritual planes must make an impact upon the consciousness of mankind, for the mind of the race is the only available instrument through which the

Divine Plan can manifest itself upon Earth. The sublimation of the world-mind is most necessary in order to heal our ailing planet, and the incoming energies of regeneration that constitute the new etheric blueprint for the construction of the New World may only be evoked by selfless and cooperative attitudes and activities.

The New World Consciousness emerging today is qualified by righteously-motivated cooperation for the common good, by altruistic example and by a purposeful dedication to serving the world. The New World Consciousness is of a gregarious nature: a *group consciousness*. Such genuine solidarity is vitally needed upon Earth as the planet is still presently dominated by a separative mind-set, and only the potency of *synergetic union* as a collective force for good can dispel the accumulated darkness of ages past, overcome global negativity, and thus manifest the present world objective.

The New World Consciousness understands that the only way to reverse mankind's suicidal course toward disaster is by using Law against law, the Higher Forces against the lower, effectively transmuting all that is obsolete and undesirable into something which is new and worthy. This is accomplished by sowing new understanding where there is ignorance, showing compassion where there is blame, returning charity for greed and by giving love in exchange for enmity. By exemplifying a united awareness, individuals who demonstrate the essential qualities of the New World Consciousness are already today introducing a higher vibrational pattern within the Earth's auric field, and the new spiritual frequencies of energy evoked in their positive activity are contributing to the restoration of our planet together with all its diverse life-forms.

Today, the first glow of the New World Consciousness is emerging in the Western world, for it is destined that the Western races will move forward in the Aquarian age into spiritual pre-eminence, without obliterating the Eastern contribution, and the functioning of the Law of Reincarnation holds a clue to this necessary cyclic pattern. The tide of life moves from east to west as moves the sun, and those souls who in past centuries excelled in Eastern mysticism, are back again today as compassionate servants of the race, happily embracing the more advanced principles and laws that pertain to Western occultism.

The Latin word 'Occultus' means *hidden*. The occult, then, is the science of that which is hidden from the five physical sense-organs and the intellect. The previous reference to occultism (and the context in which the word is used throughout this book) signifies the attainment of an intelligent understanding of universal laws and esoteric principles, and, driven by unselfish motive, a conscious wielding of the hidden forces of Nature for the good of the whole. It does not imply sorcery, black magic, lower psychism, common mediumship, etc. It is difficult for those who know nothing of the occult to realize just how great, how serious and how all-pervading are their own limitations. The understanding in the new cycle regarding the inner life and the occult dynamics of the universe of which we are an integral part, will generally be much broader than ever before, and mankind will, therefore, carry a brighter lamp of awareness throughout the world, thus helping to illuminate the road ahead for humanity.

Those who epitomize the New World Consciousness are already constructing a bridge from the old to the New. In blazing a lighted trail into the Aquarian age, they are today preparing the way for all those who choose to follow. They inspire others to take advantage of the present and unprecedented spiritual opportunity, and so help to convert current potential into a splendid reality for every person who would know success at the Harvest Time. The expansion and radiation today of the New World Consciousness, actively present in the hearts of all awakening individuals, is one very potent reality which can salvage mankind, enable humanity to move forward onto the spiritual path, and thus evoke the New Spirit which can and will build the New World. The rapid growth of networking and self-sufficient community-living around the world is already indicating how the future will unfold.

The Growing Need for Networking

ESSENTIALLY, NETWORKING IS A WORLDWIDE cooperative endeavor for the intelligent pooling and direction of resources and for the sharing of contemporary information, ideas, time, labor, etc. Today, as the knowledge of mankind is expanding exponentially due to the unfolding world-consciousness, networking is becoming a most valued priority for progress, and will be especially utilized for the efficient and expeditious facilitation of the important work of building the New World. Many persons have, up to now, been preparing in relative isolation, but are today ready to combine their efforts, for as the new world-vision makes itself known to them, they are remembering why they have incarnated upon Earth, and are, therefore, ready to offer themselves as instruments of service for the benefit of all. Such visionaries seek to invoke new and much needed light in the world, and wish to further the unfolding Divine Plan for humanity in any way that they are able.

Augmented within the new world-vision are all the established sciences (plus new ones), metaphysics, ecology, sociology, philosophy and new levels of spiritual appreciation. Together with the unveiling of previously unknown or, at best, merely suspected universal laws, all such advancements today stand in readiness to be revealed to the masses—if and when humanity becomes responsible enough to utilize them judiciously for the common good. Such important and timely knowledge will contribute toward the positive transformation of our planet and its populace and, at the right time, absolutely must be shared.

International networking promotes a global synergy, and therefore aids in hastening the necessary preparations upon the planet for the approaching transitions. The creation, coordination and purposeful utilization of networking systems, made possible by the advanced communications available today, make way for the advantageous combination of diverse but complementary assets around the world that can together be utilized to produce far greater results than if collaboration were absent.

As the awareness of mankind unfolds, new insights are yielding all kinds of useful discoveries and inventions. A growing number of new technologies available today include *free-energy generators* (which can tap the ever-accessible and limitless universal power that exists in the environment); *sonic healing devices* (which cure where orthodox medicine fails); and *anti-gravitational mechanisms* (which obviate the need for fossil-fuels to power airborne craft). *Etheric science* is revealing to the expanding consciousness of mankind metaphysical principles that have previously been known only to mystics, occultists and alchemists. *Vibrational healing* is already yielding very positive results in the civilized world, and will become the predominating and most effective medicine of the future. *Color, light and sound therapies* are becoming increasingly accepted as valid and efficacious by medical practitioners, and are, therefore, utilized today with growing success as skills improve with experimentation. Multifarious new, safe, holistic and efficient forms of healing for the body, mind and emotions abound, and more are swiftly emerging. Vital—even critical—and pioneering practical information, as well as spiritual knowledge, proliferates today as humanity enters the twenty-first century: the age of new understanding. This tiny sample of that which is new in the world is but an indication of where mankind is headed, and there are more and far greater wonders yet to be seen.

The scope of the work to be done upon Earth stands forth revealed in staggering proportions to those who, by their serviceful attitude, make contact with the new thought-projections and idea-impressions being sent into circulation by divine Agents for the helping of humanity and planet Earth. Progressively larger numbers of people today are allowing themselves to be guided, often in subtle ways, by benevolent entities who reside and operate from within the hidden worlds. Such incorporeal philanthropists seek only to be of service in order that mankind may be assisted in its necessary preparation for the coming changes, and in the reorganization and regeneration of the planet. Various useful skills and natural 'gifts' are emerging as a result of humanity's awakening. Occult powers and natural forces are being called forth intelligently by those who are able and who can be trusted to wield such energies wisely, while all benefits derived therefrom are ready to be employed today contributively within newly-instated systems of global interchange and worldwide cooperation.

So torrential is the inpouring of new and worthy conceptions at this unique time on Earth that individuals could not possibly actualize even a fraction of those creative ideas on their own and without aid. Much greater light and energy may be invoked and utilized positively for humanity by communal, national and international cooperation. *People need one another,* and as soon as just a small increase in the percentage of the race begins to truly appreciate the untold advantages of working together for a selfless cause, then, ensuing under the Law of Synergy, great accomplishments will be known—worldwide, and not only in those key areas of enlightened activity. Such is the promise of the new age, and such is the immediate goal of the Divine Plan for Earth today.

We are moving toward a *new utopia*. As both awareness and ingenuity expand globally, and as the horizon of our current potential in service opens wide before us, those of us who have set our sights upon the New World are becoming illumined by our true and practical vision that networking is a most prudent and logical step forward for the human race. From such useful public sharing, and in the name of true progress, it is concurrently being more widely recognized that local cooperative and communal living presents a sensible and most desirable development from networking.

The Rise of Cooperative Communities

THE COMING UPHEAVALS WILL GREATLY AFFECT all societies worldwide. One observation soon to be made by humanity will be the inevitable disruption and eventual collapse of conventional methods of trade, together with the cessation of the production of those deleterious and unnecessary luxuries that mankind enjoys today, e.g., those which are based upon the exploitation of diminishing natural resources, those which produce pollutants in the manufacturing process, and those products that necessitate the infliction of cruelty and slaughter within the animal kingdom. The tendency to extend commerce across large distances and internationally in order merely to appease human habits, tastes and desires is today being identified by the expanding global awareness as wasteful, superfluous and, moreover, detrimental to balanced and healthy living.

One of the greatest original factors that contributed toward separation, iniquity, suffering and disease in modern society was the invention of money, and consequently a very active trading climate that fostered tendencies toward greed, ownership, power and conflict. The societal financial systems today conduce toward worldwide domination of the many by the few wealthy and influential. Where a monetary system exists and is exploited by greed—as it has been for so long all around the world—monopoly, corruption, manipulation, injustice, decadence and consequent suffering will always follow closely behind.

In the words of Timothy: *"We brought nothing into this world, and it is certain that we can carry nothing out, and having food and raiment let us be here with content. But they that will be rich fall into temptation and a snare, and into many foolish and hurtful lusts which drown men in destruction and perdition; for the love of money is the root of all evil."*

However, there exist today alternatives that are able to replace the monetary systems, and so remedy the problems created by world trade and its associated misdemeanors. One such alternative is the *equitable bartering system* which is completely free of monetary exchange. New methods such as these have already been established and are operating successfully in certain communities throughout the world. In the near future, and following the total collapse of the world's false economies, all humanity will be coerced to utilize such alternative means. However, those who possess a true vision of the coming changes and needed adjustments are already today reverting back to more traditional values of sustenance and sharing, for they are most aware that a period of time approaches when community and cooperative living will be essential to the survival of the race.

As the old methods of livelihood decline toward eventual demise during the coming years, those with foresight will pull together in order to support one another throughout the transition period. Their clear apprehension of the future will reveal to them that a gradual and calculated renunciation of everything of the old will prepare them in stages for the necessary, final and complete abandonment of all ineffective social, economic and political systems in exchange for that which is new and better. Such trailblazers are already today beginning to demonstrate new ways of subsistence, and they are using a *new currency*.

Universal law guarantees that success will be known when a number of sincerely dedicated people work together with enthusiasm, perseverance and a common, unselfish focus, for such truly spiritual activity is in alignment with the Universal Activity. Spiritual communities are today remembering that there are sure occult methods whereby they may manifest anything that they need for the collective good. When groups of committed people can love enough, together they are able to create an *ethereal conduit* that draws energy from the higher dimensions, and this can manifest upon the physical plane in whatever form is required to further their work. It is LOVE that is the *new currency* of the Aquarian age, and to be without this currency during the coming times is to be entirely destitute.

Applicable throughout the birth of the New World, and in accordance with the new laws of the Aquarian age, the following statement of fact will be evidenced everywhere: *should an individual be unprepared to happily and spontaneously give of everything that he is able in order to serve the common good; if there is any measure of fear, self-regard and, therefore, reservation in that person, then they necessarily exclude themselves from the ranks of the true servants of the world, and so they cannot be a part of the One Divine Work upon Earth today. There can be no compromise in genuine spiritual service. Furthermore, in the times ahead, all that which is held to oneself; anything that is not offered selflessly in service to others, and everything which is not contributed toward the One Great Cause will be taken away.* Such is an often overlooked, yet integral part of the divine Promise made to humanity long ago and which is shortly to be realized by all those who love.

Presently, new communities are materializing all across the world, and these may begin with only two trusting parties. Kindred souls are being attracted to such incipient communities by their working focus, magnetic vibration and by the Law of Karma. Simple living and high thinking will allow these communities to enjoy natural, healthy and purposeful lifestyles in which the spirit of children and adults alike may be lovingly nurtured. Awakening members of the human family are today taking responsibility for providing conducive environments and effective educational systems in which the souls of children may be encouraged to unfold and grow naturally, and whereby their personalities may remain entirely free of becoming conditioned and impaired by the imposed attitudes and rulings of social systems which are themselves constricted, tainted and governed by erroneous beliefs, outworn traditions and inappropriate methods.

For decades and up to date, unusually evolved souls have been and are still incarnating upon Earth in loving response to the world's dire need for help. They are the precursors of the future new teachers[*] of the race, and are here to assist mankind in making its necessary preparations for the Great Transition. Such spiritually advanced individuals understand well how to promote the natural development of children on all levels—physical, emotional, psychological and especially spiritual—while avoiding the unnecessary pain and struggle that has been unfortunately experienced by the majority of young people in the past who have been conditioned and moulded by society with its focus upon material

---

[*] It should be noted that those who are waiting to recognize their own preconditioned idea of the ideal and perfect spiritual teacher—as portrayed perhaps by the serene and graceful personalities of the saints of past religions and biographies—are likely to miss the opportunities offered by the necessarily more rigorous and demanding new teachers of the race who are typically compelled to greet the planetary deadline having successfully contributed toward as large a harvest as possible. The subject of servants of the race, their purpose in incarnating at this time, their origins, qualities, duties, life patterns, etc. have been detailed in a book entitled *Servers of the Divine Plan: the Destiny of Ages is Nigh* (see end of book).

achievement. The new teachers are here today to lead the way forward, and members of humanity who recognize the present world-crisis and who possess some discernment of current needs will join and collaborate with these strategically-incarnating servants of mankind, and will thereby construct new and efficient communal foundations for a much more salutary way of life.

The builders of the New World shall take and utilize the best from the past, synthesizing it with the new in order to prepare for the spiritual prosperity of the coming Aquarian generation. Societies in the New World shall be thus beneficently fostered and so given the opportunity to realize a greater potential for becoming spiritual civilizations. The future of the planet rests in the hands of mankind today. However, neither in hopes for the future nor regrets about the past is the present built. The current and pressing need in the world is for the awakening to action of those who possess the vision, spirit and heart-felt aspiration to create havens for refuge and preparation during the coming storm, and who also possess the initiative and willingness to foster that which is new, life-giving and contributive toward the healing and upliftment of humanity and planet Earth.

Conversely, no community will survive during and after the tribulations unless it is built and maintained upon the sure and sturdy foundations of a joint spiritual aspiration and a selfless ethic. True community resides in the hearts of its members as a *spiritual attitude*, and not as some external objective or even a common desire to attain it. Therefore, communities in the new era may consist only of true friends; that is to say, individuals who, having attained a united awareness, do not look to one another for personal advantage, but who instead naturally and joyfully set their gaze outward and upward in the same direction for the good of the group and, of course, mankind, thus exemplifying divine friendship.

It should be understood that, contrary to popular belief and during the transition period, communities having the most far-reaching and beneficent influence will *not* be primarily healing centers; they will be centers of spiritual service bearing many different functions, only one of which shall be personal healing. It is the responsibility of genuine spiritual communities to offer a field of service to those who wish to help raise the planetary consciousness by purifying their own. Selfless service, in raising the vibratory rate of consciousness, induces a process of transmutation and necessarily confers comprehensive healing, yet does not focus solely upon it, and this is a vital key to success during the birth of the New World. Healing is an integral part of any truly divine work, but should it be the prime focus of any community, then such a center will be extremely limited from the start, for there is something of far greater moment than personal healing and which is calling humanity today from divine spheres.

Following the efficient, logical framework exemplified by all successful esoteric schools of the past, the occult structure of *Light Centers* in the Aquarian age will incorporate inner and outer circles. These concentric rings of serviceful activity will reflect the degree of spiritual attainment and, therefore, capabilities of those souls that work within their boundaries. In accordance with their own abilities, level of commitment, purity of motive and merit, aspirants will be naturally drawn inward towards those groups who demonstrate greater spiritual influence and responsibility. Each man will find the appropriate position or office that will present the best opportunities for him, while simultaneously harmonizing with the group purpose and, therefore, the good of the entire community.

It should be emphasized that the function and format of spiritual communities in the New World will be utterly unlike the various educational bodies that exist today, for the Aquarian age is not a time for workshops, courses and lectures; it is an era of *active participation* for the common good. So many *words* have been spoken and recorded for the masses throughout history by the greatest teachers, yet still selfishness, immorality and disease are rampant upon Earth. During the past, and in its selfish spiritual passivity, humanity has generally failed to learn important lessons, the karmic result of which has been so much pain and suffering. However, yesterday's tragedies do not count for naught, for they have not gone unnoticed, and growing numbers of people today *are* moving forward toward actively devoting their lives to something beautiful, meaningful and very worthwhile. In such expedient activity they are realizing that the result of genuine dedication to a valuable group-cause is inspiration, healing, purpose, fulfilment and therefore harmony and happiness, irrespective of environing conditions; true happiness and joy is an inner state, not an externally-dependent condition.

Humanity is inherently a gregarious species, yet for so long it has harbored a separative and therefore abnormal way of life which has clearly threatened both the race and the planet with destruction. It is time for us to awaken and arise from our living death, to stop taking and looking for what we can procure for ourselves, and to begin experiencing the true Spirit of life by *giving* of what we have for the benefit of all, be it time, energy, support, money, skill and most importantly love, and this in order to initiate steps toward the manifestation and active realization of fellowship on Earth.

Balanced and spiritually progressive living may only be realized through selfless expression and the giving of love and understanding to all alike. Today, this fact is beginning to dawn upon the minds of mankind as an inspired and practical vision of the future New World requirements. Empathic and responsive altruism is becoming an overwhelming motivation of, as yet a small, but steadily growing minority; a minority, nonetheless, that shall constitute the critical mass, lead the way and change the world.

Throughout eternity there can be no escape from relationship, from constant interplay between person and person, soul and soul, life and life. *Success and survival during the birth of the New World is a question of US, not I.* In earnest, loving collaboration, individual strengths and assets are used to benefit the whole community; resources are pooled, and the experience, knowledge, skill etc. of one person becomes accessible to everyone else. This is just one of the benefits being realized today by those sincere groups who are working together toward a common goal, and this globally-expanding pattern is in perfect accord with the great stream of transitions that are preceding the birth of the Aquarian age.

Those individuals who are consciously attuning to all that is new today are finding themselves polarizing positively toward seeking to be of service to others. Motivations born of spiritual understanding and based upon a shared vision of future world-unity are impelling all members of the new societal fellowships toward whole-hearted cooperation. Those members of humanity who will emerge triumphant in the New World shall tread the path together, helping one another toward the realization of a life of balance, rapport and unity. Their life pattern and expression may be analogously compared to that of healthy brain-cells working symbiotically as one greater and singularly focused creative mind.

Union is harmony and strength, and well-regulated and simultaneous efforts always produce wonders. This has been the secret of all successful associations, communities and civilizations throughout history. We may carefully regard the astonishing accomplishments achieved by the ant and bee colonies as an example of the very real possibilities that can be actualized by a one-pointed group mind. The question may arise, however: can we, or should we, really model our lives upon the crude examples given by insects!? Well, why not? *"As above, so below,"* and, therefore, as below, so above! Ants and bees have been exemplifying a vital universal principle to mankind for millions of years, ever since our Planetary Hierarchy—the spiritual Guardians of humanity—first arrived upon this planet in order to govern and hasten progress in the mineral, vegetable, animal and human kingdoms. Together with wheat, ants and bees were introduced to Earth by these exalted spiritual luminaries, and it may be prudent to consider that such enlightened beings would certainly act for definite reasons. Perhaps it is time—and indeed an opportune one today—for humanity to take heed of those examples that were left for us eons ago.

Mankind's destiny is already inscribed within the ancient pages of the Divine Plan for Earth, and thus it is known that all those awakened ones in the new era will exemplify to humanity how to live consciously as one creative intelligence, coalescing in accord with the universal Law of Unity. As heralds of the new human race, they will thus personify the forthcoming Divinity in manifestation upon Earth, and such souls are awakening today in remembrance of their duty to mankind. Their common directives and activities will reflect the structure and collective functional mode of all the great spiritual Intelligences who are actively serving the Divine Plan throughout the universe; they are the seeds for the future efflorescence of living super-social entities that are destined to flourish upon Earth in the Aquarian age.

It is through such divine societies that congenial environments for the ultimate planetary diffusion of the New World Consciousness will be fostered, and through which the physical incarnation of the spiritual Hierarchy of Great Souls will help to precipitate and maintain true fellowship upon Earth. Communal living may be rightfully seen, therefore, as an integral part of an ineffably vast and glorious blueprint conceived within the Universal Mind itself long ago. This Plan is now beginning to be appreciated and applied by mankind upon the physical plane again, just as it has been successfully by various old and even ancient civilizations of the past, only at the end of this present major cycle the whole world will join together in the sweetest chorus ever sung upon Earth: a divine hymn of united purpose and global cooperation.

The New Race

AS THE PLANET PREPARES TO MAKE its destined evolutionary leap, a new, more highly evolved human race is emerging. As previously mentioned, a great influx of advanced beings have been and are still today incarnating upon Earth in order to aid in birthing the Aquarian generation and to exemplify a new way of living to mankind. Unity consciousness is the hallmark of these accomplished souls and, therefore, similarly the person in the New World.

A special and distinguishing mark of a member of the new race is a recognition of the great need for unity, that prime ingredient that enables spiritual fellowship to be realized, and which necessitates discrimination, compassion and self-sacrifice. The essence of action by the new race will be the union of many to achieve a single and humanitarian goal, not the dominance by one who is looked up to as a guru or savior. Those who lead will do so with a group-consciousness and so with empathy, insight and love, which will impel their philanthropic activity. Understanding and compassion have ever guaranteed spiritual success, and working with, rather than against others will be the mode of operation in the Aquarian age. The forerunners of the new race—those who have incarnated to exemplify the New World Consciousness—will demonstrate a synthesizing spirit, being disposed to unite diversity of opinion and of character, able to gather around them the most unlike elements and blend them into a working whole for the collective good.

The propensities of the new race include a natural, rapid and sympathetic response to suffering, power to comprehend principles easily, quick intuitions and keen perceptions. Thoroughness, sensitivity, a sharp sense of justice and dedication to truth and righteousness are amongst their virtues, as are natural happiness, a contemplative intelligence, a pronounced passion to learn, and an eagerness to help others. Essential spiritual qualities are more naturally demonstrated, and growing from this there is a liberality of tolerance, as well as loving understanding. All that is narrow and exclusive, all that tends to separate one from another, that emphasizes differences instead of likenesses, is the antithesis of the person in the New World.

The new humanity emerging today is equipped with special senses, among them being those of perceiving the nature of the emotions and thoughts of others, and clairvoyant and prescient faculties are more developed in them than has generally been the case heretofore. Therefore, the techniques of developing the consciousness of mankind in the next planetary phase of development will be more advanced than those used in the past. They will not be the same as those hitherto employed in the East, which have motivated the new teachings that are today emerging in the West. This does not mean that the earlier methods were not correct or appropriate. It is such that the capabilities and understanding of the person in the Aquarian age are so relatively advanced that the past methods simply no longer apply to them, just as the fundamentals of arithmetic taught in elementary school fail to aid in the progress of the college graduate. These preparatory lessons were necessary in the early stages; the power or the ability to divide, subtract, multiply and add were conferred, but it is the *power* and the *ability* that are now being used by the new race, and not the exercises. These developed faculties, together with true spiritual understanding, are used not in efforts made toward self-advancement, but in service to humanity and the world.

The intuitive love prevalent amidst the new race will employ the developed intellect of mankind to build a new civilization that shall be based upon the ideals of equity and harmony. The society in the New World, being in close sympathy and rapport with the higher spiritual planes, will be very sensitive to those divine forces liberated during and after the planetary cleansing. It will readily receive the new energies that shall reinforce and stimulate it to fresh and positive impetus. The work of the new race will thus increase, this being reflected in an expansion of its breed and in the spread of goodwill, charity, altruism and international peaceful association. In summary, then, it may be said that the new race will bring into the world intuition, love and wisdom, while yet blending all that is best of the intellect and the emotion of the past races.

A New Way

IN ORDER THAT THE AFOREMENTIONED NEW RACE may flourish upon earth and for the promise of the New World Consciousness to be realized, it may be observed that humanity is presently in need of some drastic changes from its existing and long-established selfish and separative tendencies. A new way of living must be found; a true spirit of unconditional love must be nurtured. It is, however, no longer anticipated that mankind will, by itself, make these necessary adjustments, and today extremely potent forces are poised in readiness to effect the salvation and complete restoration of our planet. For the unprepared and resistant to that which is new, these forces will necessarily present much difficulty, while those who possess a selfless attitude will be stimulated and exceptionally blessed by the incoming streams of energy, and they will naturally gravitate toward the new way of life in the Aquarian age.

Due to the radical subtle and physical alchemy that is currently transpiring upon planet Earth, a new and genuine spirituality is naturally dawning within the expanding consciousness of a portion of humanity. Never before has there been such marvelous potential for spiritual unfoldment for those with unselfish motives. A new way of being is possible for each and every person today who seeks to attain or who already possesses right understanding and a virtuous disposition, and all those who would take maximum benefit from the divine forces made available in these times will find themselves expediently treading the right road that will guarantee their safe passage into the New World. Thus so, they will be embarking upon a sure method of preparation and they will be ready to receive the impending descent of the Aquarian grace which they will be naturally motivated to share with others.

The new way of relating to others and the world in the Aquarian age is hinted at in the following excerpt from an unnamed ancient scripture: *"When the Sun progresses into the mansion of the serving man, the way of life takes the place of the way of work. Then the tree of life grows until its branches shelter all the sons of men. The building of the Temple and the carrying of the stones cease. The growing trees are seen; the buildings disappear. Let the Sun pass into its appointed place and in this day and generation attend ye to the roots of growth."*

Today's aspiring individual ever lives the life of serviceful activity and of intense and simultaneous spiritual seeking, reflection and inner work. Such an example is characteristic of the person who is in alignment with the new world-paradigm in contradistinction to the old world aspirant, who escapes from life into the silent places and away from the pressures of daily living and constant contact with others. The task of those who will usher in the New World by demonstrating the new way is much more difficult, but their achievements and rewards will be still greater, and this is to be expected as a necessary part of world-progress under the auspices of the Divine Plan.

Those who find it difficult to accept that there can be a new way of spiritual growth for the world are reasonably justified. Many quite rightfully ask themselves: how is it that ancient tried and tested spiritual techniques, doctrines, philosophies, etc. can become suddenly outmoded? Well, the Truth itself never changes, but world-consciousness, perception, understanding and therefore the application of that Truth are ever being modified and adapted to the present-day requirements. A new consciousness requires a new presentation and implementation of the Truth, and hence a new way. This does not mean that established spiritual practices like prayer, meditation, yoga, etc. suddenly become ineffectual; to the contrary, the expanding inflow of divine grace may bless the solitary practitioner also, if only to a limited degree when compared to the new way of spiritual group-activity, and only if one's practice is selflessly motivated.

It is ever the *motive* behind a thought or an act that influences one's vibratory rate and, therefore, affects the purity of consciousness, and this is especially applicable amidst today's intensifying psychic climate. Mantras chanted for personal gain, prayers made in selfish appeal, spiritual practices exercised not for others but for oneself alone, and even rituals performed for self-protection will all attract negative energies to the individual, both from the surrounding environment and from within. This is because the energies that have in past been successfully utilized by aspirants seeking self-improvement are now being withdrawn as the whole planet enters its next and highest level of expression. During the coming years a continuing decline in levels of well-being will be experienced by both patients *and* practitioners who harbor self-regard, no matter how advanced they may be in their practice, for like attracts like, and the Law of Attraction is today much enhanced in its tangible effects.

It should be understood, then, that at this time having personal motives for self-advancement is not only antagonistic to the true spiritual goal of the aspirant but is also neglectful of the bountiful advantages made available today through righteous invocation in earnest groups. Selfish spirituality is imitation spirituality and spells exclusion from the emancipating joy of the way to new light through spiritual group-activity, altruism and service: the distinctive keynote of the new way in the Aquarian age, and if this is insufficient to firmly encourage the religious hopeful to reconsider his self-oriented inclinations, then he may wish to bear in mind also that in the years ahead any self-seeking will draw the old and unwholesome energies to him.

Conversely, group spiritual progress is a virtually fail-safe protection against many kinds of religious delusion. If two or more people are working together earnestly for the benefit of all, the pitfalls, illusions and egotistic impulses that are so often found upon the path of self-liberation may be seen and uprooted by another sincere member of the group as they arise. Each new seed of delusion is thus given little chance to take root in the fertile soil of the ego, while simultaneously, spiritual merit is at hand as one group member helps another.

Group—not individual—spiritual growth is the new way. The current needs of humanity, the opportunity to contribute, and the inestimable value of intelligent and earnest group-collaboration must be recognized by all those aspirants who wish to enter the New World. The essential questions to be considered in order to gauge whether we shall qualify for group work and, therefore, spiritual opportunity today should be: are we ready to adjust ourselves to the present need and to sacrifice personal desire for something much greater in order to serve the cause of the Divine Plan in this, its present phase? And are we ready to build for a brighter future, together, for the collective good?

The new Aquarian age is upon us, and the integration of mankind warrants definite changes in technique though not, of course, in the most basic and spiritual goals of life. The following adjusted law of the new age should be clearly understood by awakening humanity: *upon the understanding response to the collective needs of mankind will depend the rapidity with which each individual will be enabled to achieve the next revelation and expansion of consciousness which is, for him, possible.* Each of us has, therefore, to consider our individual response to the demands of our own spirit, and our collective response to the collective need. All candidates for the forthcoming spiritual opportunity are now appealed to by mankind's invisible Guides for this united service.

Spirited motivation for group collaboration and joint service will naturally follow a realization of the world's urgent need, a recognition of the Divine Plan, and an apprehension of the immediate point of world attainment. This in turn will evoke the consequent investment of the total of one's resources into the furtherance of the One Divine Work upon Earth. When our insistence upon making the transition out of the lower (personal) and into the higher (divine) life has been felt within the inner worlds by those who watch and wait, and when our pledge to our own soul that we shall allow no impediment to deter our resolution for service has been noted, assistance will be given by divine Agents. Under the laws of the Aquarian age, *such assistance is given only to those who have transcended selfish aspiration and lost sight of their own progress in the genuine and selfless impulse to be of service to others.*

The word goes forth to the spiritual aspirants of today who are bound for success: lose sight of self in joint-endeavor, forget personal desire in group-activity, pass through the portal into new life in group-formation, and let the personality life be lost in the greater Life of spiritual inclusivity. Thus, the New World precept of spiritual progress through collective service will be realized, a principle that has for ages been observed upon the hidden side of life, and under which Earth's Hierarchy of Elders have happily progressed while aiding and protecting their younger brothers and sisters: humanity.

Today, the appointed emissaries of many different interstellar alliances continue to incarnate upon the physical plane on Earth in merciful answer to the prayers and needs of humanity. They are presently finding their positions, and will soon exemplify that the Law of Service is the governing law of the future for planet Earth. In past ages it has been the service of one's own soul, with the emphasis upon one's own individual salvation, that engrossed the attention of the spiritual aspirant; naught else was considered. Then came the period wherein the service of a spiritual master, or guru, and also of one's own soul, was considered of dominant interest; the master was served and duty to him emphasized, because thereby the salvation of the individual was aided. *Now a new note is sounding forth in the world, the note of growth through the service of the race*, through cultivated self-forgetfulness and through group-communion with the Divine. Teachers and gurus are not utilized today in the same unthinking and acquiescent way as in past times, for the Truth is now being sought and found directly within while in active group-service.

As we are moving forward into an era of greater intelligence, dogmatic belief and blind faith are becoming redundant in the revealing light of true understanding, direct knowing and spiritual experience. The true and innermost impulse of mankind has ever been to serve and obey the Greater Self—the Spirit—and this is beginning to be more widely appreciated today. In the past, however, this simple truth has been distorted by church authorities, extremists, fundamentalists, scholars, etc., and has produced the multifarious formulas of spiritual philosophy and religious theology. These formulas veil the Truth; they have been presented to the consideration of mankind in terms of personality devotions and of obedience to masters, leaders, deities, religious systems and established organizations instead of fidelity and service to the One Spirit in all. Such false presentations of the Ageless Wisdom must and will change in the Aquarian age, and it will be appreciated that spiritual insight, expanding vision, intelligent and positive control of one's destiny and the development of consciousness are the results of efforts made by using one's own initiative; never have they been the outcome of blindly following the recommendations of others or their doctrines.

The grasping nature of many prayers, based as they are upon personal desire, are regarded as disturbing, impractical and inexpedient by a growing proliferation of those who recognize the truth today. The vagueness of meditations taught and practiced both in the East and in the West, and their emphatically selfish note, e.g., to gain peace, liberation for oneself, personal healing and empowerment, etc. is likewise causing frustration and revolt for want of something bearing greater wholeness and spiritual substance. The order of the day is not for personal enlightenment, nor even the search for greater personal happiness, but for intelligent preparation for the imminent world-initiation.

Today's intensifying psychic climate demands united effort, group-understanding, cooperative service, group-contact with the Divine, collective salvation, and integrated relationship with the soul in one another and with the Greater Self in all. Indeed, *if group-collaboration is absent; if the true team-spirit is not being demonstrated today, then there is not much that the divine Helpers of the race upon the inner side of life can do for humanity in these unique times.*

For many cycles, the spiritual Hierarchy has been withdrawn into an apparent silence upon the higher levels of our planetary sphere where contact has had to be made with them by aspirants who have, by discipline, spiritual development and service, qualified themselves to establish such a relationship. Today, however, circumstances are very different. New inflowing energies and the ongoing thinning of the veil between worlds have made a closer relationship with Divinity possible to a greater number of human beings than in the past.

The spiritual Guides of the race, then, are today much more accessible from within than has generally been the case heretofore upon Earth. Contact with them by the earnest seeker may be made in various ways: it may arise from simply reading a book containing important seeds of truth, which might catalyze a more receptive state of consciousness; it may present itself spontaneously as a synchronicity, a vision, a silent inner sense or an impression relayed via one's own soul. Contact may be received in symbolic form while in meditation, or in dreams, which can be analyzed and comprehended upon due reflection. Guidance might be witnessed as an incentive, a sudden inspiration or dynamic and compelling impulse in the life of the person contacted, or it may be registered as a flash of intuitive understanding revealing a larger part of the nature of Reality. Such a revelation may effect a greater appreciation of future possibilities, potential destiny and the need for service in our times; it may even reveal the overall purpose of a person's incarnation, and thus stimulate the conscious aspiration toward the successful consummation of one's life-mission. Whatever form communication with these inner Teachers may take, it will never encourage the individual to become dependent upon anyone or anything, but will always facilitate personal divine contact and will advocate group-collaboration for the good of the whole.

Many are at last hearkening to the New Spirit's great urge for change. Humanity is being called to awaken and to embrace a new and much better way of life. Conscious groups are today drawing upon divine forces to bring safely into the world much greater light for all. The invocational potency of light and grace in these unified groups is enormously greater than that which may be known individually, as was assured two thousand years ago when the Christ said, *"When two or more people come together in my name, I shall be there with them."* Due to the present influx of cosmic energy in our solar system, group potential is unparalleled today and continues to expand. The principle of synergy that is applicable only in sincere and dedicated group-work shall contribute toward rapid group- and world-awakening like never before upon Earth.

It would be most prudent indeed not to overlook the incredible potential for group spiritual unfoldment in the new age; no traditional spiritual practices are needed (yet may, of course, be helpful). The new energies are utilized for group-awakening by the active application of informed and appropriate attitudes toward that which is relevant today. The why and how of attunement to the new frequencies must be understood by all those who would arise joyously into the New Light. Conscientious attention should be given to the following statement by all serious spiritual aspirants: *the portal of initiation leading to the New World may only be traversed in group formation; such is a law of the Aquarian age.*

Equipped with true understanding and its corollary: intelligent surrender, dedicated groups are today completely trusting the divine Intelligence within themselves. Thus so, and in accord with universal law, ever present and benign spiritual forces are made available to them. Pledged members of such groups are naturally allowing all personal concerns to effortlessly dissolve in the joy and security of group-communion, while simultaneously activating an invisible channel within the center of the group through which these forces may flow. Inevitably, grace streams forth from the higher worlds and through such purposefully-constructed conduits of spiritual blessing, thereby illuminating the consciousness and opening the hearts of those present. Such a process catalyses the rapid transmutation of all gross auric energies, thereby releasing psycho-emotional blockages and producing various healing wonders as it leads to emancipation from worldly pain and suffering. The unselfish and intelligent use of such a powerful method of conducting divine energy in these favorable times gives rise to the construction of a potent ethereal circuit that blazes a stream of electric force through every opened heart and bestows Revelation upon the whole group as each individual's consciousness fuses and unites with the group-mind and is subsequently lifted into luminous spiritual realms where the experience of unconditional love for everyone and everything is known.

But this is not all; indeed, it is only the beginning, for in activating the Law of Invocation synergetically within the group, the corresponding influx of divine force will not only uplift and sanctify the consciousness of those responsible for its induction, but will proceed to radiate positive, healing and pacifying energy outwards from the center, simultaneously effecting the transmutation of negative energies in the surrounding environment by purifying, healing and vivifying all the kingdoms of life on Earth: mineral, vegetable, animal and, of course, human. Such auspicious activity is in part responsible for the summoning, anchoring and worldwide distribution of the new Aquarian frequencies of light-energy, and it is this new way that shall be exemplified in the emerging esoteric schools that will be publicly recognized and respected in the New World.

Humanity's readiness today to step forward onto a higher turn of the spiral—the path of group spiritual development—is a very positive sign indeed, for it reflects an important and inevitable universal process whereby individuality merges back into the Oneness of the Divine. Such unification is the ultimate goal of all sentient beings within every sphere of Creation, and it is this one great objective toward which the driving thrust of the Holy Spirit eternally urges all life.

The Sinister Side of the New Age

WITH ALL THE GREAT POTENTIAL for unprecedented light and rapid spiritual progress in the world today, it is of little surprise to note that the forces of selfishness are also particularly engrossed in their own kind of work upon Earth. They are, once again as always, vying for attention by perpetrating all kinds of guileful antics as they endeavor to gain for themselves as much attention and power as they are able to grasp. The age-old struggle between good and evil is again evincing itself here upon Earth, and is, to a growing number of awakening individuals, especially noticeable today as the dawning light of the New Day is throwing shadows in all directions.

As greater light continues to illuminate the planetary consciousness, darkness is necessarily accentuated; where there is light there must exist its corresponding shadow, or contrast, for in a dualistic universe one cannot exist and is meaningless without the other. More specifically, there has existed for millions of years a great protective barrier of spiritual force around our planet that was instigated and has been dutifully maintained by the Earth's own planetary Hierarchy. This ethereal bulwark regulates the incoming flow of various energies, forces and souls to Earth, while it also functions as a shield from cosmic evil. Without such a measure humanity would have experienced much greater oppression and hardship than that which it has known heretofore. In this time leading up to the birth of the New World, certain *doorways* are being opened in the barrier in order to allow for a larger influx of benign entities into our Earthly sphere where their aid may be rendered. However, these doorways are presently also being used for access by entities who are rather less than friendly! Nevertheless, such undivine souls have the karmic right to be here on Earth.

Such entities are representatives of primeval and malevolent powers that still exist in the universe, and today, as ever, they are striving toward effecting stagnation in the world as they invariably seek to retard progress by fostering craving for self and attachment to the known. They work effectively through the selfishness of personal desire, fear, pride and conservative attitudes. Such ancient materialistic forces have ever been pitted against true, spiritual advancement, and thus they are in conflict with the flow of the Spirit which, like a stream, is ever changing, ever new.

The forces of darkness incorporate very real and wilful intelligences who work to preserve that which is old and material, hence they are pre-eminently the forces of crystallization, or of form-preservation. They promote the attractiveness of matter, desire for temporal control and power, and the lure of that which exists in the form-life of the lower worlds. Consequently they deliberately attempt to block the influx of anything that is good, true and life-enhancing, as greater divine light certainly threatens their dominion upon Earth. They do this by distorting the new truths and by stimulating desire and excitement in offering false substitutes that may appear to be new and promising, but which are, in fact, only re-presentations of the old ways of self-gratification. Principally, and whenever they are able, they endeavor to preserve that which is familiar and old, to counteract the effects of the oncoming culture and civilization, to bring confusion to humanity, and to feed steadily the existing fires of separateness, criticism, animosity, etc. These forces work insidiously and cloak their efforts in fair words, leading even sincere spiritual aspirants to feel and express antipathy for certain persons and ideologies, thereby fostering the hidden seeds of hatred to be found in many human beings. They fan to fury the fear and antagonism of the world in an effort to maintain that which is outmoded; they make the unknown and true appear undesirable or unbelievable, and they attempt to hold back progress for their own ends.

Now, essentially there is no evil in this world, no vice, no sin, except for that which flows from the assertion of the individual self. The propensity of self is to cling to the known, and most people in the world today tend toward the old, the fixed and the 'secure.' Such is the general disposition of humanity into which its social-conditioning and extremely limited education—so painfully devoid of the greater verities of life—have programmed it. The vast majority, then, have become steeped in the ignorance of egotism, and resistance to change is normal for them. However, as purifying forces pour into the subtle energy fields of our planet, the darkness of old, ingrained delusions and selfishness in all their diverse forms are being forced up and out like the poison in a wound. All anxieties, fears and other occult contaminants that obscure the light of the Spirit are necessarily surfacing in our lives today; the true colors of humanity are beginning to be clearly exposed, and there is much more yet to be revealed in a changing world that is struggling to be free of all inharmonious influence.

Equipped with an adequate understanding of the world situation during its current process of purification, we would all do well to remember the fact that if the mind makes a practice of rectitude in its thinking, then there is no evil that can make entrance into it. However, a growing number of people today *are* being impressed negatively (and most often unconsciously) by antagonistic forces in order to thwart or to completely quash anything that is supportive of the successful unfoldment of this current phase of the Divine Plan for mankind. Such sinister manipulation is greatly facilitated by individuals who harbor fearful or selfish attitudes and motives, and the forces of darkness who are recruiting today for the 'final battle of Armageddon' are certainly not restricted in their choice of prospective candidates on Earth! Agents of evil are often quickly recognizable, but sometimes manage successfully to conceal themselves, for example, beneath the pious mask of religious philosophy or spiritual idealism. *"The devil quotes scriptures for his own designs,"* and the person who would know the truth must be especially vigilant today amidst the proliferating wiles and illusions that are being consciously perpetrated upon our planet, mostly from hidden spheres. We must learn to recognize and pick out the spiritual wheat from the emotional chaff, bearing in mind always, especially in these exceptional times, that there exists in the world a great deal more chaff than wheat!

Today, as stimulating psychic forces are unleashed and made available to mankind on an unprecedented scale, the unsuspecting, hasty and unenlightened are exhibiting their new abilities with remarkable alacrity, prematurely stepping forward to inaugurate themselves to the general public as spiritual teachers, healers and masters of wisdom, when in reality they have only made contact with the *astral plane*. These uninformed and unwary innocents are most often quite blind to the very real dangers of untrained lower psychism (e.g., clairvoyance, mediumship, etc.), its powerful tendency to tempt, consequently inhibit or even to cause a regression of real spiritual progress. They are also usually quite unaware of the potential that astralism inherently possesses for attracting the interest of cunning spirit-beings who simply love to cause as much mischief as they can in these important times of global catharsis and transformation.

In being aware of the expanding light upon the horizon of the New World, the forces of darkness are today redoubling their efforts against the Forces of Truth by trying all kinds of new, devious and desperate attempts to further delay the unfolding

Divine Plan, and to take for themselves as much of the new light coming to the planet as they are able to snatch away from humanity. In order to ensure greater success in their goal the dark forces often offer fake spiritual gems that may appear to sparkle in the beginning, but soon fade and become lackluster, along with the temporary satisfaction that may have been initially gleaned from them.

If a true divine experience has yet to be attained, the exuberant and hopeful self-seeker may easily confuse astralism and psychic phenomena for spiritual revelation and holy wisdom. If a person with desire of any kind decides to meddle upon the lower astral plane (which is readily accessible to many today), perhaps seeking to contact discarnate entities thereupon, they throw open wide the door of their consciousness for mischievous and evil forces to freely enter in. This is especially so for teachers who demonstrate influence over others, for in their commanding and, therefore, powerful position they become prime targets for the cravings and ambitions of lowly-evolved and maligned spirits. Such beings seek to contaminate the minds of their unsuspecting victims with their delusory ploys as they simultaneously draw attention and life-force to themselves. The majority of these discarnate souls are quite unhappy, and since misery loves company they endeavor to render such damage as they are able by imposing their own will through the passive consciousness of the unwitting medium. Such treacherous patterns are evidenced today among many New Age groups, and are spreading like an epidemic due to an absence of basic occult understanding, humility, and that purity of intent which is essential for safe and useful psychical work.

It should be understood that there is a limitless abundance of intriguing facts (and falsities) that are accessible upon the astral plane by its legions of residents. Such information often seems impressive, and may appear bright and true to those who grasp blindly for something new and exciting, and indeed, on occasion, a jewel of truth might slip through.[*] However, the astral land is known in esoteric circles as the *realm of illusion*, partly because its

---

[*] Due recognition is given to the fact that some accurate and very useful information is presently being received through *bona fide* mediums. However, it should not be overlooked that this is only *information*. Mediumship (or 'channeling' as it is usually called today), in and of itself, does not constitute a path of spiritual development.

lower sub-planes provide residence for egotistic denizens who are often much less evolved than their mediums, and who have desires and designs of their own. Truth is often corrupted by such entities either innocently or wilfully, prior to being subsequently tainted by the illusory nature of the astral plane itself, and finally also by the personality of the medium. The result: the great plethora of exaggeration, misinformation and imitation spirituality in the world today. Due to the extant ignorance of mankind and the intensity of the period, mediumship is currently proving itself to be more often a curse than a gift.

If messages from lofty spiritual planes are to be reliably and accurately conveyed through a medium, then the impression must be a direct descent from higher mental levels to the brain, avoiding all contact with impurities in the astral (emotional) part of the medium's constitution. Only in so far as this direct descent is attained will the recorded impression be devoid of error; it will not then be tinctured with any emotional complex whatsoever. For it is the astral level of consciousness that is the great distorter of essential truth. True interpretation of messages from the higher worlds is dependent upon detachment from lower psychism. The medium must be essentially humble, and so personality-decentralization is an utmost requirement for true, safe and successful spiritual mediumship. This is critical today as more and more mediums are being targeted by the dark forces.

Often mediums are aware at some level that their 'guides' have at least some personal motives that are not entirely divine, yet these mediums continue to follow their instructions at the expense of complete integrity due to their own lack of discrimination, fear of ridicule from their established students, and sometimes for far more unscrupulous reasons. Many established spiritual leaders, teachers and gurus are, to the perceptive observer, conspicuously falling today, and so exemplify to the children of the New World that blind and unintelligent submission to external authorities is inherently dangerous and strongly inadvisable. In fact, the real and qualified spiritual teachers in the Aquarian age will not gather disciples around themselves. The perennial admonitions solemnly given by sages of yore would especially profit everyone at this time and ought to be revived and retained in the minds of all those who would safely tread the spiritual path today, for *the pharisee is often further from the kingdom of God than the publican and the sinner.* In every way unholy company should be avoided by the seeker of Truth because it will likely give rise to passion, glamour, excitement, contagion, blindness, false hopes, delusion, etc., and all at a cost to wise decision and real spiritual progress. Psychic experiences may seem at first a bubbling froth of something better, but they veil one's eyes and serve only to inhibit higher perception.

Presently all over the world there exists an overabundance of new religious institutions, spiritual societies and esoteric organizations that have allegedly been inspired and guided by contact with great masters, Christ-like entities, highly advanced extraterrestrial light-beings, and even angels and archangels. While it is true that a far greater profusion of very evolved divine Agents are closer to Earth at this time than ever before in its history, it should be born in mind that so is the opposition: the antichrist,* and the devotees of any spirit-beings, their teachings or their nominated representatives would do well to remember always the occult dictum that states *like attracts like*, for this is an immutable universal law. The

---

* The antichrist is not a single person or being; it is not the 'Devil' or 'Satan,' neither of whom actually exist, although a great number of entities continue to derive satisfaction from impersonating the mythical Lord of Darkness. The term 'antichrist' refers to all evil intelligence as it is expressed in the universe in direct opposition to the plans of the Cosmic Christ—*The Lord of the World*—who is not the personality called Jesus, but an extremely exalted field of divine Consciousness, a Great Being of Love and Wisdom, one tiny ray from whom shone through the lower vehicles of Jesus, as it did through those of the *Avatar* Krishna of India, before him, as well as many other great Servants throughout human history, thereby bestowing upon these individuals the spiritual title of *world-savior*. The word 'Christ' is derived from the Greek 'Kristos' meaning *The Anointed One*. Those who work under the banner of the antichrist include a whole host of sentient beings, some of whom are very advanced in terms of their occult knowledge, their power to control certain lesser spirits, and their ability to wield various natural forces; others may be quite unaware of how they are secretly used by the brothers of shadow, but all of them have one thing in common: selfishness, while those of a more treacherous nature harbor an insatiable lust for power, personal aggrandizement and dominion over others. It is, in fact, their innate selfishness that prevents any real and permanent alliance among them, and this is why the forces of darkness are always ultimately defeated by the greater united power of those who serve the Divine Plan, and who constitute, therefore, the divine Forces of Righteousness.

level of morality, virtue, humility and, therefore, the frequency of consciousness of the medium who makes contact upon the inner planes dictates the spiritual class and delimits the caliber of the channeled entity. The average desire-bound individual will certainly not be chosen as an agent upon Earth to convey the sacred and momentous messages of lofty spiritual beings, although such mediums may easily misinterpret their distorted thought-forms within the astral worlds, which are but broken reflections from higher spheres.

Today, an inordinate mass of ordinary people bearing minimal spiritual development are claiming to be the officially appointed channels for the authentic new teachings of various exalted beings, many of whom have become well known via various established religions for thousands of years. Gautama Buddha, the Lord Maitreya (Christ) and even God Himself! are to be heard speaking through an unlikely assortment of mediums today. Such nonsense exemplifies the great sham within the New Age movement, even though the printed material collated from channeling sessions and enthusiastically distributed by those who wholeheartedly believe in it, may appear to be dependable, authoritative and even somewhat uplifting. It should not be overlooked, however, that even a young, dull and mischievous child is able to quote pleasantly-sounding axioms or make false promises, and the astral plane is copiously littered with the shards of discarded thoughts and ideas from ages past and up to date, ready to be taken up by any vagrant spirit who happens to be wandering by.

Highly advanced spiritual beings generally do not limit themselves by communicating at the level of the individual personality. They typically influence many different souls simultaneously, and their communications, which operate under the Law of Impression, are effected upon higher levels of consciousness, where very few mediums today are consciously able to reach due to their personal desires, which necessarily limit their contact to the lower astral plane. The great Guides of the race have ever served humanity by way of an ancient, highly organized and intricate hierarchical system comprising many exalted lives, masters, high-initiates, disciples and worthy emissaries who have all proven their spiritual merit by successfully emerging from the fires of past trials and severe tests taken over numerous incarnations.

At this time all around the world it is a common occurrence that yesterday's office clerk or manual worker is magically transformed into today's 'enlightened teacher,' and such absurdities lucidly illustrate that *psychism is not a sanction for true, spiritual work*, and that *psychic ability does not necessarily (or even usually) correspond to spiritual purity;* nor does it indicate advanced mystical attainment (which must be realized through long and diligent practice) be it of the white or the black magician. It is a noteworthy fact that domestic pets such as cats and dogs are psychic, as are members of various primitive tribes located in Africa, South America and elsewhere.

A great number of species of animals are generally more psychic than human beings because, while remaining completely free of the constricting and obstructive psychologies that mankind so prevalently possesses and demonstrates, these animals are naturally and effortlessly sensitive to the thoughts and feelings of other sentient beings around them. Such members of the animal kingdom regularly communicate psychically with one another, and they can sense changes and presences that arise within the subtle planes that exist alongside our physical world.

Psychism is a most ordinary and natural function, but humanity generally desensitizes itself to these inherent and latent abilities due to a compulsive and emphatic use of the lower psyche, and the consequent development of a rigid mind-set that may include all kinds of limiting false conceptions, fears and prejudices. Due to its unnatural and habitual tendencies, therefore, the human race has to date generally and subconsciously opted to close down its psychic awareness, while those few who in the past have chosen to freely demonstrate their uncommon psychic abilities, in attracting the wrong kind of attention, may have landed themselves in serious trouble.

Throughout modern history fear has been the chief motivating force behind the suppression, persecution and even execution of those who evidenced psychic powers, e.g., witch-burning in the middle-ages, the Spanish Inquisition, etc., and many psychically sensitive individuals have been promptly treated as insane. Today, however, the energies of the Aquarian age are forcing open previously inhibited channels of psychic perception and sensitivity in mankind, and the world is no longer able to deny these very real faculties due to their emergence and demonstration *en masse*. However, due to the pervasive lack of occult understanding amongst humanity, lower psychic faculties are currently being misused and abused, while the misconceptions born of New Age psychism continue to mislead many. Lacking right understanding in these times we shall be like the blind man in *the valley of the shadow of death*. Occult education is critically required today in order to prevent individuals from falling prey to those identical temptations that have led to the total destruction of whole civilizations upon Earth in the past.

Channeling, as it is still widely practiced in its lowest and most material form, is a low grade psychic expression. It is, for the masses, definitely one of the least demanding 'spiritual paths'; it is easy and therefore of negligible positive influence upon real spiritual progress. In stark contrast, divine-contact has ever been the most important and prime goal of the serious spiritual aspirant, and this rule has not changed merely due to the increased psychic sensitivity in the world. Being the most direct communication with the Spirit for humanity, divine-contact facilitates the receipt of pure insight, flawless intuition and dependable wisdom, obviating the need to contact other beings for information. It will also allow for the beneficent radiation (via the personality) of the light of the Spirit, the nature of which is intelligent, impersonal Love. Conversely, channeling can be very detrimental to the individual upon the spiritual path for numerous reasons, and once divine-contact has been attained becomes completely superfluous.

Channeling, therefore, constitutes a definite distraction to real spiritual attainment, and for the average person today is fraught with danger. Moreover, the trance condition that many lesser mediums effortlessly adopt is a most undesirable state, especially in these times. It separates the medium from their own soul, and definitely relegates them to the realm of uncontrolled and material forces that abound upon the astral plane. It is imperative that mental activity be enhanced and selflessly dedicated to helping others so that intelligent and conscious channeling may be practiced safely if at all, otherwise true, spiritual mediumship will remain a rare occurrence within the New Age spiritualistic movement. The naïveté and excited grasping of the majority of those who are interested in channeling, together with the ingenuousness, pride and selfishness of the bulk of mediums, exposes groups to very definite dangers as they continue to let loose in the world forces and entities of an unholy nature.

All manner of devious spirits are today proceeding to seek out and to contact sensitives in physical incarnation who evidence reasonable potential to become instruments for the execution of their ungracious plans, just as the benevolent and true Servants of the race are searching for selfless and devoted hearts to help with the real Divine Work upon Earth. As the lower psychic faculties of mankind expand, dark forces may eagerly rush in where angels will not tread. Wherever there exists even a tiny blot upon the motives of the medium, he or she is automatically prone to be surreptitiously deceived, used, victimized and even permanently possessed. Conditions are so ripe at this time in the world and humanity's gullibility and desire so pronounced and prevalent, that such unfortunate occult usurpations are being facilitated by a negative synergy actualized by unprepared groups of perhaps well-meaning people. This is resulting in group-possessions and it is to be observed today that certain mediums together with some of their loyal followers are headed straight for the lunatic asylum!

Lowly-evolved and unscrupulous entities bearing sinister ambitions recognize how easily they may outwit unsuspecting human beings. Many of these wily disembodied spirits are no great fools, and they understand well that the dissemination of alluring but erroneous teachings may seem authentic and dependable to the unwary on account of the truth that lies at the base of them and which is intentionally allowed to slip through their falsifications. For it is the little bit of truth in an error that gives it its appeal and strength, not the great wrapping of falsehood that overlies the scrap of truth, and many teachings being given out today are gross embellishments or distortions of basically sound contemporary facts. How many hopefuls will become most embarrassed, if not sorely grieved, when they eventually come to realize that their beloved master or lofty angelic source is no more than a deceased human personality of low order, or even merely a rather bold and mischievous nature-spirit!

The previous illustration is a characteristic example (and not, by far, the most shocking) of that which is transpiring within the New Age movement today, and it is everywhere apparent. Large, affluent, fully-established, well-attended and even 'prestigious' spiritual organizations exist around the world that have been instigated due to the communications and manipulations of entities with, at best, unquestionably deluded motivations. Many of those who are presently offering false teachings are all the more convincing to the unaware due to the fact that they themselves actually believe what they teach, and may therefore possess genuinely sincere motives. Yet while they forge ahead with the notion that they really are serving the Divine Plan, they are in fact little more than human marionettes for masters of deception who work from within the hidden worlds. It is one of evil's favorite and most frequently employed ruses to pose as holy messengers, for it knows well how to appeal to humanity's pride and desire. These dark spirits are well-practiced and skilled at masquerading their true intentions with a facade of stimulating and evocative melodramas and emotionally appealing beguilements of all kinds.

By way of their chosen human instruments on the physical plane, the forces of darkness may perform miraculous healings and demonstrate psychic powers in order to inspire faith in the masses, and to subsequently win the adulation and allegiance of the naïve. What may be regarded as miraculous by some, however, is nothing but a metaphysical dynamic that is responsible for the harnessing of natural forces; faith acts as both a magnifier and a conductor, and makes this dynamic possible. Just as electricity—which is potentially present everywhere—becomes effective only in the presence of a conductor, so 'supernatural' power becomes effective only in the presence of faith, be it faith in a human teacher, in the divine Intelligence immanent in Creation, faith in an ideal or even in one's own spiritual nature. History attests to the fact that blind faith may be easily and promptly cultivated amongst the credulous, desirous or needy. Furthermore, those cunning entities who are sworn enemies of Truth and Righteousness understand very well how selfishly-motivated faith may be exploited and used like a kind of vacuum that draws certain surrounding forces into itself, thus endowing the individual or group with which it is connected with various etheric and astral energies that are naught but imitations of those higher forces in which the faith has been invested.

It is a fact that in order to instigate and maintain their power and charisma, spiritual and religious leaders depend as much on the faith of their adherents as their adherents depend on the initial inspiration which they may receive from their leaders. Once this mutually-profitable affair has begun, it can easily expand to allure and subsequently influence many other aspirants who may be attracted (or magnetically pulled in) to the psychically-charged atmosphere that is so common within such groups. The subsequent and rapid magnification of synergetic potency will be in direct proportion to the degree of emotional charge peculiar to the group, as well as the will and manipulative abilities of the leader(s), and it is not difficult to see how the combined forces evoked by those whose faith is directed toward a spiritual 'superior' make him a center of power that goes far beyond that of his own personality, while simultaneously also providing a convenient conduit for other evil minds to enter and influence our world.

Religious intermediaries are still employed today due to humanity's ignorance of universal laws, and as long as such blindness persists in the world, black magicians, false spiritual leaders and bogus religions will continue to proliferate in response to mankind's desire. A rapidly growing number of false prophets and unscrupulous mystical teachers are rising in power around the world today. Due to the pervasive ingenuousness and craving of humanity, these sorcerers are successfully wielding occult forces not for the common good, but for their own selfish ends, and they are consequently leading many people farther and farther away from the truth and genuine divine experience by offering a *cold light*, which can be remarkably convincing to those who do not look to their own heart for verification.

Upon entering the charged atmosphere of certain congregations the sensitive person may soon become aware of an upliftment of mood or psychic stimulation of some kind, while beneath such a cunning enticement the more vigilant newcomer may witness an obscure sensation that betrays the fact that some external force is attempting to mesmerically impose its influence and to instigate control. Often, certain ceremonies or meditations that are regularly performed by members of the assembly will—consciously or unwittingly—facilitate such possession or, in the case of the weak-willed, vacant-minded or needy, even guarantee the successful attachment of some disembodied being (or group of beings) to the aura of the unsuspecting optimist, with the preconceived purpose of eventually working its way into the nervous system and the brain of the victim. This depiction may seem rather morbid or even fantastic to the uninformed, yet the reader who lacks sound occult knowledge is assured that this is usually only the initial introduction to the intended insidious career of the possessing entity.

Where opportunity is presented, misguided discarnate spirits are today purposefully breaking divine law by enticing or coercing the souls of some individuals to vacate their bodies, usually temporarily but on occasion permanently, in order to inhabit them thereafter, wherein they endeavor to influence others. Such occult possession is becoming a common occurrence in the world and is made easy by those who succumb to fits of passion such as anger or lust, or who allow themselves to yield to other traits of the lower self such as jealousy, lying, self-pity, depression, hatred, fear, habitual condemnation of others, etc., etc.

Each individual, and no one else, is wholly responsible for all the conditions within their own reality, for these conditions exist primarily in their auric field as the energies that they have created by their thoughts and emotions. The key to safety and success during this dark eve of the New Day lies within the heart. Negative and selfish thinking, however, is especially hazardous in these 'testing times' and bears the terrible potential to attract entities who dwell amidst the hordes of maligned spirits who are today being forced up against the physical plane by the Forces of Righteousness, which are battling victoriously upon the other side of the veil between worlds. These now frenzied dark wraiths are desperately seeking their impossible escape from the dazzling light of Justice by fleeing into physical human vehicles. It is a fact that there are many more 'walk-ins' of questionable character alive today upon Earth than there are truly holy visitors. However, it should be remembered that for every single soul of purity and wisdom, one thousand or more evil ones may be offset, and many such bright souls are presently moving into position for the forthcoming and conclusive confrontation that will ultimately manifest in the physical world.

※ ※ ※

Aside from the more severe dangers of lower psychism, it should ever be born in mind that psychics who are lacking in sound occult training, track-record and purity of motive cannot and should not be trusted to convey accurately the truth of the times. Proclaimed spiritual teachers should always be thoroughly tested for their moral standing, their depth of esoteric knowledge and their past genuine experience in holy service, and this before any iota of allegiance to them or their methods is even considered. False spiritual teachers are today disseminating all kinds of intriguing information in their attempt to distract the masses from the simple, unchanging and spiritually sound message of love and service. The Holy Truth is, has ever been and always will be—simple, and complexity often spells danger. The well known ancient Chinese curse may be regarded today as a warning: *"May you live in interesting times."*

Those beings who operate within the ranks of the forces of darkness always work along the path of least resistance. The devil is characteristically a most lazy fellow whenever he can afford to be! He has ever been most disposed to advantage himself from any method that seems likely to further his insidious cause and which appears to promise him the least amount of trouble or labor. Today he is exploiting with ease the ignorant nature of human beings, while artfully employing the rampant glamour and exaggeration within the New Age movement to ensnare as many hopefuls as he can. At the same time he is, with very little effort, using that same glamour to deter many of the thinking people of the world from apprehending the real facts. Sceptics today are rather hastily and eagerly condemning New Age thinking in its entirety as 'mass-hypnosis,' 'group-infatuation,' etc., and this is because they have observed only the nonsensical side, which is by far the larger part, and which, admittedly, is saturated with so much fuss, excitement and credulous obsession.

Today's pervasive hype and glamour has resulted in much smugness, excitement and pride, and this is exactly what the dark forces intended. Due to the abundant and much distorted presentations of contemporary facts that have been thoughtlessly peddled by eager, naïve and self-seeking individuals during the last few decades, the sacred essence of the truths that represent the real significance of the birth of the Aquarian age have been terribly adulterated and consequently misconstrued by many. This has resulted in a great neutralization of the benefits offered to humanity in accordance with the Divine Plan for Earth. Through exaggeration, misinformed passion and unintelligent, misguided enthusiasm, important and critically-relevant information regarding the world-transformation has become hackneyed, stale and consequently improbable to the minds of many. Cliched prattle and 'spiritual marketing' by the unaware has discouraged numerous people from recognizing and responding to the urgency and magnitude of that which is today transpiring. The devil's calling card bears the same insignia as it always has, if only we would care to take a closer look. Earnest and intelligent seeking, right understanding, practical vision and active service are required today in order to offset the damage inflicted and time wasted by the plethora of falsity and ostentation that proliferates in the world with regard to the New Age.

Having thoroughly researched the spiritual supermarket for over a decade, uncompromisingly seeking full-time across four continents, it is our personal and authentic observation that at the time of writing (1995), an accurate figure denoting the proportion of bogus (or at best misguided) 'spiritual' teachers, leaders and groups at large today in our experience is 95% plus! The larger part of the New Age movement, even at its best, only manages to provide a dubious presentation of the truth of the times, while at its worst is undoubtedly sinister.

It is a most noteworthy fact that one basic truth is often used as a foundation for a great pile of deception, as is prevalently the case everywhere today upon the eve of the birth of the New World. Nevertheless, wherever there is truth to be found at all, the serious seeker will always possess the earnest and genuine spiritual impetus to probe and delve deeply within a whole mountain of lies if necessary in order to find it. And if he digs down deep enough into that great mound of falsehood, thereby discovering and bringing out the truth to set it radiating on top, then the entire mountain of lies will crumble under the weight of that single truth. Evil is essentially conservative, it simply hates being disturbed by the truth.

Fortunately, evil together with all its lies, selfishness and other egocentric tendencies may often be recognized clearly enough by discerning persons, but for those who do not yet possess discrimination, adequate esoteric knowledge or dependable intuition, pseudo-spirituality may be rather more difficult to identify. Yet egotism (which, in a sense, is synonymous with evil: the divisive factor in Creation) can always be recognized by its propensity to attack or defend for the benefit of itself. A close and uncompromising scrutiny of the character of and results obtained by any spiritual group will usually reveal the truth. However, a general guiding rule may be offered here: wherever educational groups fail to emphasize, encourage and inspire selfless service of a distinctly spiritual nature; wherever promises are made of gains for the personal self alone; or where tempting benefits are offered for the individual at all—BEWARE! The true spiritual Path must be sought for itself, and not with regard for the feet that shall tread it. Most importantly, sincere seekers should listen within rather than to the opinions of others; they should ever trust and be true to themselves, remembering always that desire blinds.

As has been assured by the disclosures presented in this book thus far, there certainly are most precious gems scattered amongst the glut of New Age paraphernalia that is available everywhere in the Western world today. Like a fine, golden thread, the truth is very subtly woven throughout the many enchantments and infatuations that lay like so much unwanted sediment upon the surface of the real contemporary facts. All those sincere and venturesome aspirants for true knowledge and understanding in these remarkable times are most heartily encouraged to make their search steadfastly, with discernment but without excessive eagerness. There are important lessons to be learned in every single experience, and we often learn much more by encountering the evils and deceptions of life's circumstances personally than we do from simply being handed truth upon a silver platter, as it were, where it might go unappreciated. Sometimes we have to quest deeply into the dragon's lair in order to retrieve essential treasures, but if the nature of evil is comprehended well enough and one's motives remain pure, then the devil together with all his cohorts may be faced with unshakable confidence. Thus assured in their certain knowledge that they will be victorious, the resolute trailblazers of the times shall detect the golden thread of Truth and will employ it wisely in order to guide themselves safely through all the present-day contrivances, until they successfully reach the center of the New Age cyclone, where they will See and Know.

The widespread rise of falsehood and darkness is a very normal occurrence at the close of cycles, and one that necessarily precedes the advent of new light in the world. This is so for various reasons, and one important purpose of such 'timely evil' is to afford humanity its needed challenges in the form of trials so that individual choice may be made. Each man is thus given opportunity to hasten his own spiritual growth and simultaneously qualify to proceed forward into a brighter era. Those who, albeit unwittingly, choose to become entangled amidst the multitudinous enticements of the transition period leading up to the Harvest Time automatically exclude themselves from entering the New World by failing to recognize and overcome the 'temptations of evil.' The sinister side of the New Age movement may ultimately be regarded, therefore, as an important factor in a necessary selection process that will permit only those pure, vigilant and worthy souls to pass through the Portal of Initiation, and to rise into the resplendence of the New World.

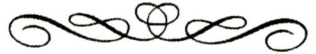

The Liberating Path of Service

WHEN WE IDENTIFY AND STRUGGLE with the problems of the personal self we cannot see a way out of our loneliness and suffering because we are looking in the wrong direction! Should we forget this most important principle of life, we need only recall to mind the existence and example of our sun, which constantly demonstrates a fundamental divine law.

As above, so below. The sun is the crown chakra of the body of our solar system, and the solar system itself is a great deity *"in which we live and move and have our being,"* as the old adage affirms. The solar deity is a *macrocosmic* example of the human microcosm, with its mental, emotional and physical vehicles of expression. Similarly, an atom is the *microcosmic* reflection of the human being and, in its turn, the sun is but a microcosmic expression of something far greater, and so it goes on unto Infinity. Through the cosmic evolutionary process, every atom is destined to become a sun and more, as the One Universal Being—God—expands eternally.

Returning to our local solar system, the same essential laws apply to both the sun and the soul of man. In observing our physical sun we might regard with due awe its natural ability to draw power from an evidently limitless source, and to subsequently bestow light, heat and other life-giving energies continually upon all creatures and forms of life within its boundaries, its body. The same applies to the human microcosm, and through the soul of man flow the vital energies that nourish and sustain all the bodily processes—subtle and physical—providing the life-force and intelligence of each cell and every single atom that constitutes the human being; thus the soul—or *personal deity*—informs and animates the very consciousness of man.

Now, the sun shines! It does not *try* to shine; it does not perform rituals, resound prayers or practice any kind of spiritual technique in order to gain something or to better itself, and it certainly does not struggle with countless personal problems, desires and fears as does humanity, and this *not doing* is the secret of its success. Conversely, in man's *personal* struggle for freedom, in his antagonistic efforts to gain happiness for the separate self, in his self-imposed separation from the true and inclusive life of the Spirit, and in his ignorant and exclusive self-regard, he is actually contravening one of life's greatest laws, and so he must pay the price. Self-orientation contracts consciousness, and in thus obstructing the light of his very own soul from irradiating and expanding his awareness, man prevents his liberation from the darkness, suffering and struggle that have been his lot for ages upon Earth.

The Law of Cause and Effect is insuperable. People become unhappy, get sick and die because in focusing upon the little self—one microscopic mote in a veritable cosmic ocean of like particles—they lose sight of the greater whole of which they, as a personality, are an intrinsic and inseparable element. Man is generally so busy in habitually transgressing universal law that he fails to *look*, to *see*, and to therefore take benefit from his macrocosmic exemplar and master: the sun. What is focused upon grows, and in the constricting focus that man chooses to maintain, he consummates his own "eternal damnation" as he separates himself indefinitely from the rest of Creation: his very own Greater Self. Thus, as long as man chooses to remain wallowing in the primeval mire of his selfish and fearful self, then his separation from God, the Fall from Grace and Lucifer's (mankind's) banishment from Paradise will be perpetuated.

Unhappiness, discord and disease are unnatural phenomena. They do not constitute part of the Universal Harmony and are not a design of the Divine Plan of Perfection. They are mankind's creations, as are all problems on Earth. With a little imagination it is not difficult to ascertain what would transpire if our sun were to follow *man's* example! And if every sun throughout the Cosmos were to do the same, then all the stars in the firmament would grow dim, flicker and die; the universe would be no more and God would expire! Today, Mother Earth is painfully close to just such a fate, and she, along with all humanity, bears testimony to the world-disharmony that we, as a race, have perpetrated in our forgetfulness of universal law. Yet the sun still shines, as it will indefinitely, just as long as it maintains its selfless focus and continues to surrender to the great Law of Love. And in recalling to mind the sun's perfect example whenever we find ourselves feeling any lack of vitality or inspiration, we may begin to reverse our downward-spiraling course into darkness by looking past the little self and into Life, by helping others, by giving to the world and by living for the greater good, just like the sun. Thus, we, too, will shine forever.

* * *

In selflessly serving the One Spirit in all—starting perhaps with our immediate friends, family, associates or our group—we shall find that our own highest needs are met by way of such service. Once the spiritual heart is thus kindled and set aflame in loving service to others, all personal problems resume their correct perspective and begin to dissolve effortlessly. For example, during times of great misfortune or disaster, the soul of humanity naturally responds to the greater needs, and thus in finding purpose through crisis our own personal problems lose their immediacy and may even cease to figure in our awareness altogether. At this present stage of human development on Earth the clarion call of the New Spirit is sounding urgently forth and is entreating every heart to willingly give up the futile search for personal gain—material or spiritual—and to look toward the greater needs of the world. It seeks to elucidate and evoke within us all the wisdom in joining hands together as one, for the sake of the realization of a larger and brighter vision for the whole planet.

The grace of the times may only be received by the virtuous, and in thus becoming illumined by the liberating Aquarian energies, an awareness of the many previously concealed yet vital lessons in life may be appreciated. When we are able to really *see*, everyone and everything becomes a reliable tutor, the Book of Nature is opened and its secrets are revealed, divine-contact is established and, therefore, intuition is awakened. True intuition always impels one to do the greatest good for the largest number of people, for if one is attuned to the Spirit via one's own soul, then one is also aligned to some degree with the Divine Plan, and the Divine Plan is, in turn, designed for the benefit of everyone. Intuition, therefore, being ever unselfish, may be rightfully regarded as *group-perception*, that is, vision afforded by attunement to divine law for the good of all. Selflessness is the golden key that will avail each person today of the greatest blessing in the world, which is given in order to be shared with others, and when the door of present opportunity is unlocked, opened and the threshold crossed, sincere aspirants will find themselves upon the Path of progressive spiritual liberation in service to their fellows.

Service may be rendered at many different levels, of course, but in order to offer true, spiritual counsel, a sound occult knowledge is essential. The greatest purpose of knowledge, once attained, is its practical application in life, for only through experience is wisdom gained. Furthermore, knowledge cannot be fully realized if kept to oneself; knowledge is for sharing. The person of knowledge who lacks a good heart is like the bee without honey, and it is a fact that the knowledge which is not shared with others eventually becomes a poison to the one who clings to it for self. However, it is an infallible universal law that when we give selflessly we receive more spiritually in return. There is a wonderful divine premium to be had in the experience of lovingly sharing higher knowledge openly with others for their good, and this is just one of the rewards found upon the Path of Service. By forgetting this simple yet foremost and eternal spiritual principle of giving, we allow ourselves to remain in the illusion of our lonely selfhood, the forces of which shall keep us deluded, maintaining our segregation and struggle for as long as we abide in our forgetfulness of our inseparable relationship to the greater whole.

The erroneous yet popular idea that a man cannot serve others adequately until he has reached a greater level of spiritual attainment—perhaps through meditation or some other discipline—is a pretext of the ego, which has always and will ever attempt to retard real progress, and is especially devious and deleterious today due to its intensified battle upon Earth with the Forces of Liberation. The ego is a seasoned liar and is exceedingly resourceful in supplying false, even if seemingly logical arguments to the conscious mind in order to hamper a person from moving forward onto the liberating Path of Service. It should be remembered that the ego always seeks to protract its own separate and selfish existence, and will do its utmost to prevent a person from effecting its dissolution by becoming selfless. Conversely, and in demanding the attention of the Spirit, loving service is the great nemesis of the ego, for it threatens its very existence, an existence that is painful because it guarantees separation and therefore suffering. Selfless service, then, is the quickest and most effective way to dissolve the illusion of the separate ego, and to consequently unite with the All.

It should ever be born in mind that there is no life activity, no vocational calling, no mental occupation, and no condition which does not provide the key with that each man may unlock the next appropriate door for himself; the door that shall usher him forth into a brighter reality and serve to lead him towards the mountain top from where a wider horizon can be seen and a larger spiritual vision attained. The key is *opportunity to serve*, and when this truth is seen it becomes clear that absolutely everyone can begin serving humbly as they are able by starting from right where they are, as all the great saints and spiritual masters have done. It all began for them with one kind thought, and these eminent benefactors of the race proceeded from there to clearly and repeatedly demonstrate to humanity that for every single flower of love and charity a person plants in their neighbor's garden, an undesirable and troublesome weed shall disappear from his own.

It has been repeatedly averred by all the religious teachings and enunciations of the great spiritual leaders throughout mankind's history that individuality is really one with the whole; it has been clearly pointed out that the belief in the illusion of a separate self and the consequent indulging thereof is the cause of all segregation and suffering. Furthermore, should we pause to reflect upon the obvious fact that an infinitely larger portion of the Cosmos exists apart from the little self, then we are likely to appreciate the relative insignificance of that self as well as the enormously greater substance, magnitude and import with regard to all that is not of the self. With this in mind the seemingly separate individual would do well to consider the wisdom of never having any interests that are opposed to the universal laws that guide and govern all Creation. Of course, the selfishness of egotism is diametrically opposed to one such law: the sacred Law of Love, and so, like one's shadow, trouble will necessarily follow the transgressor of that law. Yet the plain truth is that in helping others lies our own greatest good, and spiritual aspirants are most truly progressing when they assist the progress of their fellows.

Ancient wisdom states that the divine Helpers of the race can do little more for men than they would do for other men. The Law of Love is paradoxical to the grasping self, for Love must be given in order to be received. If we would not lose that which we have gained, then we must give it away. Loving hearts will most readily be able to enter the New World, and so all who possess real spiritual understanding today will be naturally disposed toward embarking upon the path of active service. It may be observed that genuine servers generally demonstrate a happiness and joyful spirit that is ever absent amongst all self-seeking minds. They know well that in true service the garden of the gods—humanity—unfolds and blossoms into a truer, more divine expression, and so they happily demonstrate that *the path of spiritual service is the most splendid, noble and holy way; it is the Royal Road for which all other disciplines are but preparatory.* This may be easily verified by noting how all the great spiritual teachers and leaders throughout history have trodden the path of selfless service. If there ever was one solution to absolutely every problem throughout mankind's history, all the way up to the present and on into Eternity, it must surely be . . . *serve, and keep serving; give, and never stop giving.*

* * *

For many people today there is some confusion as to who to serve and how. The solution is, however, exquisitely simple. The divine essence of all human beings, without exception, loves the Truth. Virtually every single person in the world has a divine spark in the heart, and if that indwelling life can be contacted, roused and drawn forth through the personality, then a most worthy spiritual service will have been rendered. Therefore, our spiritual service may be offered to virtually everyone we meet. Due to humanity's current need, opportunity and present stage of development, the question of *how* to serve is also very straightforward indeed, and the answer lies in your hands. Generally, the most valuable service that may be given today in this unique period is to spread the vital truth of the times and so present others with the *choice* that they must make in these last days of the cycle. Soon after this process is commenced by one who has recognized and understood that truth for themselves, and so is confident in reaching out to others with sincerity and altruistic motive, the Spirit will take over as divine-contact is established. *"Have no fear for what ye shall say, for the Holy Breath will speak through you."*—Jesus. Thus, when right understanding allows us to forget the personal self in informed consecration to the furtherance of the Divine Plan upon Earth, service upon the Path of Love becomes as effortless as it is joyful.

In devoted service our awareness of the wondrous adventure of life grows ever brighter, each moment becoming more meaningful, expansive, joyous and liberating as we are progressively illumined by the light of the Spirit. Thereafter we have little other sane choice than to continue reaching out to humanity with our emancipating inner realizations, and in thus serving others, we shall be tacitly inviting all those who would accompany us upon our return journey back to the divine Kingdom. Certain very beneficent results are always assured by genuine devotion expressed in service. These include vitality, healing, expanded awareness, joy, spiritual unfoldment, and so much more. It must be so because *service is love in action,* and is therefore governed by a supreme divine law: the Law of Love. The effects of positive causes created by selfless service are far-reaching indeed. Unlike the temporary and self-effacing results of all selfish deeds, the favorable effects of Love endure eternally, for the substance of Love constitutes the quintessence of the Universe.

When we cease in our seeking for ourselves alone, and so in knowing greater freedom from the burdens created by personal desire we are able to demonstrate compassion and goodwill to others, we open a channel for the Love of Spirit to flow through us. Love for all beings is known only upon the one True Road that leads back to Unity. Through service to mankind we shall allow that divine Love to manifest; such is the Way of the Higher Evolution, and such is the sure and only way to lasting spiritual fulfilment and happiness.

A Parable of Heaven and Hell

There once was a devoted priest who wished to see both heaven and hell, and God gave way to his pleading.

The priest found himself before a door which bore no name. He trembled as he saw it open before him into a large room where all was prepared for a feast. There was a table, and at its center a great dish of steaming food. The smell and the aroma inflamed the appetite.

Diners sat around the table with great spoons in their hands, yet they were shrieking with hunger in that terrible place. They tried to feed themselves, and gave up, cursing God, for the spoons that God had provided were so long that they could not reach their faces and get the food to their tongues. So they starved, while their dish of plenty lay amongst them. The priest knew their screams were the cries of hell, and as this understanding came, the door closed before him.

He shut his eyes in prayer and begged God to take him away from that terrible place. When he opened them again, he despaired, for the same door stood before him, the door that bore no name. Again it opened, and it gave onto the same room. Nothing had changed, and he was about to cry in horror. There was the table, and at its center the steaming dish, and around it were the same people, and in their hands the same spoons.

Yet the shrieking had gone, and the cries and the curses had changed to blessings; and nothing had changed, yet everything. For with the same long spoons they reached to each other's mouths and fed one another, and they gave thanks to God.

And as the priest heard the blessings, the door closed. He fell to his knees, and he too blessed God who had shown him the nature of heaven and hell, and the chasm — a hair's breadth wide — that divides them.

Author unknown

Keys to Awakening

AS PREVIOUSLY MENTIONED, invisible divine Agents are reaching out to humanity in blessing at this important time upon Earth like never before, and so, courtesy of these Servants of the race, keys to awakening are now readily available to every aspirant who is earnest and persevering. When the portal of spiritual opportunity is beheld by those who are in possession of the keys, together they will be able to open the *combination-lock* and to cross over the threshold into the New World. So what and where are these keys? There are many, they are diverse and, for most people today, they remain concealed. However, there are just three *Master Keys* which, once discovered and employed, will avail the sincere aspirant of all the others, and these three will now be revealed.

The first Master Key for all those who are lost in the wilderness of this wayward world is an earnest and humble attitude of SEEKING.

The Truth may only be found if it is earnestly sought, and the search for the meaning of life is something that absolutely everyone would undertake if they were not so immersed in an overabundance of worldly distractions. This is so because the impetus to seek and thus to evolve is an essential quality of the divine Spirit, and so is also inherent within the heart of every human being. To become aware of the grand possibilities of spiritual seeking is to be onto something; to fail to be onto something is to live an empty life. It may be clearly recognized, therefore, that an open and inquisitive attitude is necessary if rigidity and stagnation are to be avoided and spiritual progress assured. Such is the inborn and natural instinct of a child, without which it would never grow emotionally, mentally or spiritually. Similarly in adulthood, the seeking of greater meaning in life is essential to spiritual advancement; refraining from seeking any higher purpose other than mere survival, pleasure and procreation is to experience spiritual death.

All genuine spiritual teachers today will endeavor to stimulate a process of seeking in their students. These teachers will offer such aspirants truth, but without proof. The true seeker does not request proof from his mentor, for such an attitude is not concurrent with the spirit of genuine seeking; the spiritual thirst of the sincere seeker is both sufficient and necessary to drive him onwards unyieldingly. *"Surely it is the greatest miracle that an ordinary person may become a saint."*—Lord Buddha. Such saintliness is latent within all sleeping human beings and, in never being content to compromise upon half-truths or fleeting experiences, the serious aspirant for Knowledge and Wisdom constantly seeks the Truth, and upon its discovery is enlightened by it. The earnest candidate for spiritual understanding, then, possesses a burning and uncompromising passion to know the Truth, and thus his own process of seeking will be self-generated.

The foregoing point is vitally important because motivation along the spiritual path must, in every case, arise from within the individual, and this necessity pertains to the Law of Free Will under which human progress proceeds upon Earth. The very act of seeking sets natural forces in motion that greet the seeker in order to impart certain 'secrets' which that individual may be ready to behold; Life responds as if to an invitation. By self-initiated efforts to move forward into grander regions of spiritual reality, the intuitive faculty is automatically stimulated and the seeker's vibratory rate of consciousness is raised as his awareness expands. This process of spiritual advancement is significantly hastened if one's search is made with an unselfish attitude, i.e., not for oneself alone, but for the benefit of the world. Rapid progress is assured upon the Path of Service, which intrinsically requires an unassuming attitude of seeking, and this *Path of Return* has been marked out by all the great Teachers who have successfully trodden the same Way before, and so to follow their trail is to go forth to reunite with the Divine.

The search for Truth is the most wonderful and magical journey in the world and constitutes the essential first step toward revelation and spiritual success. Earnest and intelligent seeking is an especially indispensable quality during the birth of the Aquarian age, and is also an integral and inseparable part of the New World Consciousness. It engenders inner contact with divine Agents and the Greater Self, who shall willingly offer their impeccable guidance to ensure a safe journey into the New World.

Those aspirants who will know victory during the times ahead do not seek to, and neither do they wish to be seen to do great things, and for just this reason and due to their natural humility, they are able to accomplish them. From their dedicated seeking and harmonious alignment with universal law, they gain an unshakable confidence in the perfection and invincibility of the Divine Plan to which they consequently pledge their whole-hearted allegiance. Therefore, they share the patience of the Spirit, being without the eager, grasping haste of personal desire. Nonetheless, the successful seeker is no fool and will persevere upon his quest intelligently; he will utilize all available tools and aids along his chosen path. One such aid, and a very useful second Master Key for some, is MEDITATION.

Contrary to common misunderstanding, meditation is not merely a formal sitting practice of concentration. When the focused mind is fully and steadily directed toward any object, idea or activity for a due length of time, thereby piercing the veil of illusion and uniting with the inner or hidden reality—the Greater Life to which the mind belongs—then meditation is performed. Therefore, one accurate definition of meditation is: *focused attention upon life.*

The highest goal of formal meditation practice, through the establishing of a calm, mental receptivity and inner spiritual contact, is to gain an empathic understanding of life and the realization of at-one-ment with it. Once such awareness is achieved and retained, a person will be most adequately qualified as well as compelled to reach out to his fellows and to lead them from the darkness and confusion that their separated selfhood has imposed upon them, back into the light for which their souls yearn. Therefore, it may be recognized that meditation is ultimately performed *for others*, and should this understanding be the prime motivating factor for one's practice, so much the better, for such a noble and truly spiritual attitude will enable a person to attain his goal most expeditiously.

Formal meditation begins with the practice of concentration (or focused attention), bearing an attitude of detachment from results and a passive acceptance of whatever presents itself to the mind of the observer. One's practice need not be anything grandiose or special, in fact the greater its simplicity the better. Calm, one-pointed attention upon a single object, mantra, idea, principle, quality or even a bodily process such as breathing is sufficient.

By regularly practicing simple techniques of meditation, daily and not necessarily for a long time, the answers to life's mysteries may be received from within. Indeed, in true meditation all questions ultimately dissolve, leaving one extremely simple yet profound universal verity, namely that Love is the greatest aid to spiritual emancipation which, in turn, is the purpose of life. Once this truth has been realized, the meditator will be ready to embark wholeheartedly upon the path of selfless giving and to joyfully serve, just as other great souls have served and are now serving upon the planet. Regularity and detachment from results, then, are the keys to success in meditation.

Meditation is a tool, a means to an end. Prior to the meditative state of consciousness becoming natural and constant, its formal practice should not be the sole focus of one's existence to the exclusion of the other many opportunities and duties that abound in life. Meditation, like any other obsession, will become a curse to the clinging mind, and every serious aspirant should always remember well that balance is the prescription for and the gift of the truly spiritual life.

It should be noted that not everyone requires a regular or formal practice of meditation (although nearly all will benefit from this in some way). There is a very simple formula that may ascertain the appropriateness of meditation for each individual: if meditation yields some benefit, e.g., a greater level of contentment, insight, serenity or even more restful sleep, then the practice is well-suited. However, if one's practice tends to elicit adverse effects in any way, then such an exercise should be discontinued and perhaps another technique found. Each individual should always do that which makes him feel happy and uplifted. Never should any practice be coerced at the expense of well-being and amiability, as is so often evidenced among the anxious, self-seeking or idealistic.

During the coming upheavals, free time will be much restricted, and formal meditation for long periods will become both impractical and inexpedient as active and coordinated attention to the needs of each moment will be demanded by the surrounding tumultuous circumstances. This will inevitably engross the full attention of every meditator alike, be they a priest, mystic, monk or yogi. The dynamic changes in the near future will absolutely coerce each individual to become very practical, which means that *going within* as a meditative habit will necessarily shift to an attentive external focus. Remember, however, that the definition of meditation is not merely the withdrawing from the exterior world to look solely to inner realities. The outer world is an equally worthy object of concentration, and even though it is generally much more challenging, accomplishments in terms of superior benefit for all may be proportionally greater than those that may be gained by practicing in isolation.

It is useful to note that the world's most accomplished meditators have always emerged from their solitude in order to extend their meditation in service to the world, and theirs may be said to be the most supreme meditation of all, for it reflects the one great and eternal Meditation that endures within the Heart of the Universe itself, and has done ever since the blueprints for the

Cosmos were conceived, i.e., even before its creation: a very long time indeed! Thus, the meditation of service appears to have been quite adequately tried, tested, successfully demonstrated and so verified as being a most pre-eminent practice, and this certification has been made by a rather Higher Authority than any teacher upon Earth.

Seeking and meditation, then, lead to the all-important understanding that shall consequently reveal that active SERVICE is the most significant of the three Master Keys, and of greater importance to the aspirant even than dedicated formal meditation. This is so because it is the earnest and truly selfless activity of the individual that evokes the powers of the Spirit, brings about the intensification of the divine life, and leads, in a graded series of steps, to the *Great Renunciation*, which sets the server eternally free from the illusion of matter.

A few words ought to be mentioned here regarding what service is *not*. Lacking true spiritual understanding, which is gained only by earnestly seeking, some who may like to think of themselves as philanthropists proceed to serve based only upon a theory of service, which is, however, deeply covered by their own personal interests, desires, ambitions, etc. and is therefore fuelled principally by ulterior and selfish motives. This is perfectly demonstrated by those who cling self-righteously to some ideal, dogma, system or organizational decree, and who seek to impose their beliefs upon others in the name of charity. This they do under the guise of selfless service, yet upon closer inspection it may become apparent that their real and underlying motives are not altruistic at all, and that they serve perhaps only to gain confirmation of their beliefs, for self-satisfaction, to establish some level of influence or control over others, or merely to appease their own conscience. Such pseudo service can and does produce much harm and confusion in the world, for people often attempt to force their ideas of service and their personal techniques upon others who may blindly follow the more commanding, yet erroneous, conviction of those who appear to know better.

'Love' for the majority of people today is not really Love at all, but a mixture of the *desire* to love and to *be* loved (or acknowledged in some way), plus a willingness to do anything to show and evoke this sentiment, and consequently to be more comfortable in one's own life. It is this pseudo-love, based upon a theory of love and service, that characterizes so many quasi-philanthropic endeavors and human relationships; yet neither theory, personal aspiration nor desire will or can ever make of a person a real server. In past, much emphasis has been laid upon that which is interpreted by most as 'Love,' and not enough has been placed upon *Wisdom*, which is Love expressing itself in service. True service is determined only by the pure motive that prompts the server's activity. True service is rendered by the spontaneous outpouring of a loving heart together with the direction of an intelligent and dedicated mind. It is produced by the inevitable inflow of spiritual force from the Greater Self via the soul due to the unconditional goodwill of a person, and not by strenuous physical-plane activity or by the studied effects of the server's words or deeds. It may be thus recognized that all true spiritual service is rendered by the Spirit, not the temporal personality through which the Spirit seeks to express itself. True servers work in self-forgetfulness, offering up their vehicle of consciousness—the personality—for use by Divinity; they give no thought to the magnitude or the reverse of their accomplishments, for they are genuinely concerned for the well-being of others. They bear no preconceived ideas as to their own value or usefulness, but live, work, serve and aid, asking nothing for themselves. In fact, the thought of reward is completely unnecessary, and the aware servant of all knows this as he works under the infallible auspices of the Law of Recompense, whereby all is awarded and balanced perfectly and appropriately.

As yet few people realize that as far as the ego is concerned, genuine spiritual service is often destructive. This is necessarily so because old attachments, erroneous belief systems and false securities must be effaced in order that the light of a new and greater truth may illuminate the awareness. Consequently, true servers are frequently misunderstood upon Earth, for the love that they express differs widely from the sentimental, affectionate and personal interest of the average person. They are necessarily occupied mainly with the spiritual prosperity of all humanity as a race, as well, of course, as all life. They are not primarily concerned with the petty interests of individuals who are predominantly occupied with their own little problems and concerns. Such impersonality regularly brings servers under the criticism of others and, consequently, they may find that they possess very few friends. However, they will always know who their real friends are, for upon the spiritual path in the Aquarian age, genuine servers of the Divine Plan will stand as one in group-formation, looking out (of the personal) and upwards in the same direction.

When a man discovers the spiritual life and truly begins to live it, seeing all as equal and ceasing to identify with the illusions of duality, e.g., good and bad, better or worse, pleasant and undesirable, etc., he necessarily become impersonal. The eyes of the Spirit, which can truly see, are utterly impersonal. Now, it may be recalled that like attracts like, and when a man becomes spiritually aware the world of ego is bound to reject him. This illustrates a universal principle that functions under the Laws of Attraction and Repulsion. As the path becomes narrower and steeper, so the numbers walking it diminish. However, provided they live by what is true and maintain it to the glory of the divine Spirit, the devoted server will be entirely indifferent as to whether he personally loses or gains everything, for the one who in all things is truly bold in his allegiance to the Divine Plan will be as ready to do the one thing as the other, and always with joy, for he comprehends well the wonderful Law.

There is a major issue to consider at this time, which is of the greatest importance for all those who have yet to commence some serviceful activity, but who decidedly wish to enter the New World, and that is the matter of preparation for service; for *all who would cross the threshold between the old and the New and emerge into the magnificence of the Aquarian age on Earth must possess a genuine love of others and, therefore, an attitude that naturally impels their wish to be of service.* Today, those who seek to render such service must recognize universal law, the significance of the period in which we live, and its adjusted requirements for spiritual success during the challenging times ahead.

Those who are already guaranteed of a successful graduation during the coming Harvest Time know well from experience that upon selflessly and appropriately sharing with others that which has been revealed to them, more is given from within. Such is just one blessing bestowed upon those who attune themselves to the Law of Service, the utmost law for mankind's spiritual progress in the new cycle.

The three Master Keys to awakening during the birth of the New World, then, are: sincere and intelligent spiritual SEEKING, MEDITATION for the greater good, and, most importantly, active and selfless SERVICE. Additionally, many minor but essential keys will be discovered upon the path once the Master Keys are utilized well. These will include: the comprehension of and attunement to new, adjusted or existing natural laws and vital Aquarian energies, which are intrinsic to the spiritual life in the new age; the reaping of invaluable advantages from freshly-presented knowledge, teachings and wisdom; the participation in the joy of spiritual sharing and, of course, the new and vitalizing realization of harmonious and meaningful new ways of living. All these keys and many more are accessible to every intelligent person today, and will ultimately lead the serious aspirant to a good understanding and application in their lives of the new way of conscious spiritual growth which, in turn, will permit them successful entrance into the New World. In addition, those in possession of the keys to awakening will be awarded the most gracious honor of our times, namely that of assisting others in attaining success at the Harvest Time.

* * *

An all-important key-attitude for adoption today embraces the realization that it is time to become very fluid, like a stream that completely accepts and yields to its surroundings in order to flow unimpeded as it meanders onward in a smooth and uninterrupted movement. Such a resilient disposition will highlight the expediency of discarding as many desires and plans as possible, and of fostering trust in the guiding wisdom of the Spirit in order to effortlessly follow its sure direction in each new moment. A recognition of the whispered messages from the Spirit within can be assured by remembering one very elementary fact: one's state of consciousness will rise upon doing something appropriate and good, or deteriorate when doing something that is at least potentially detrimental to the greater good, and thus unfavorable for the individual also.

Useful habits to establish for the great journey into the New World are those that inspire joy and which feel natural, ever bearing in mind that philosophically-sound ideals that might have worked well yesterday may today be inappropriate. All serious aspirants are strongly recommended to trust their own feelings and higher senses much more than they may have done in the past, and also to be true to themselves, for the *still small voice within* is necessarily growing louder in these important times. During the approaching critical period, the birth-pains of the emerging New World shall be known to all, and we shall certainly flounder without our divine Shepherd to guide us safely and appropriately. Therefore, we should learn now to listen well to our own, often subtle, yet infallible inner guidance.

Further keys will be entrusted to humanity depending upon its positive response to those opportunities that have already been offered. An important law of the Aquarian age decrees that more grace from hidden quarters will be made available only after that which has previously been given by divine Agents is seen by them to be utilized well by the recipient in service to others.

> *The full set of keys to awakening have been dexterously concealed by unseen Hands within all of life's experiences, yet such tactical and clandestine measures present no barriers to the dauntless adventurer. The bold seeker is quite aware that the Secret Treasure Chest of the present golden opportunity lies awaiting discovery by the diligent, uncompromising and, therefore, worthy soul who has embarked upon the True Quest, found the all-important keys along his tortuous path, and who has finally reached the center of what at first seemed to be an enigmatic and complex labyrinth. It is he who, unremitting in his thirst to know the Truth, shall unveil the Mystery of the New Age and unearth the most rare of bounties known to mankind. Bearing the rightful keys obtained through his toils, pains, sacrifice, experience and skilful passage, he shall be eligible to unlock the Ancient Clasp that binds and protects the Great Prize, thereby releasing new light into the world. In now being well-practiced at following obediently the unfaltering guidance of his own inner voice, he shall, with a sprightliness born of true, spiritual inspiration, venture upwards from the great underground catacombs of his past trials, pushing forward far beyond his previous limitations, while watching in delight as all previous illusions dissolve. Bearing a gracious and loving smile reflected outwards from deep within himself, and imbued by a radiance and transcendental exultation unknown to him before, the hero will emerge from darkness perfectly in time to greet the blinding glory of the New Dawn, and to share his new-found fortune, with everyone.*

Just so, the present period, with its magnificent opportunities made available to all humanity might be depicted in symbolic and mystical-fantasy form, yet it takes just a little discernment to recognize that such an apparently fanciful allegory is most befitting and clearly representative of the potential reality evidenced in these exceptional times.

The Most Important Message

NOT ONLY DOES THE INFORMATION contained within this book rank amongst the most momentous in the world today, but its expositions are also timely, auspicious and of great value. The discerning reader will see that this remark is not merely a prideful claim made by ourselves for our own vision (a vision which is now revealing itself to many others around the world), but is an obvious fact, for never before has there been such an occasion and eminent opportunity as that which is today offered to humanity and which is expounded herein. An adequate understanding of the very real potential during the period leading up to the most important Harvest Time ever upon Earth may inspire every person to effect the appropriate action that shall ultimately avail them of the tender-sweet fruit of the long-awaited divine Promise: *Deliverance*.

Those who are informed and aware will certainly not wish to allow themselves to become complacent, however, even as they discern the impending resplendence of the New World, for they know that there is much commitment and expedient cooperation required of them, both today and continually leading up to the Great Transition itself. It is a fact that every time the planetary bell tolls announcing the opening of the gateway to a new age, every time there is a tendency toward synthesis and new understanding in the world, every time a lesser reality is about to be merged in a greater, and every time new universal ideas begin to make their impact upon the minds and within the hearts of the masses, there ensues a subsequent upheaval or cataclysm, a breaking down of the old and of all that which might prevent those ideas from becoming anchored in physical-plane reality. Therefore, never before has there been such an impending spiritual opportunity, yet at the same time never before has mankind faced such a great challenge.

Today's new opportunities and challenges are directly related to the all-important approaching Harvest Time, and this period of drastic change is affecting, and will continue to affect to greater degrees, all of the kingdoms upon Earth: mineral, vegetable, animal and human. In the human kingdom, perception of time is shifting as the transformation of world-consciousness advances. The manifestation of planetary, national and personal karma is speeding up as causal seeds sown long ago and heretofore are surfacing in order to be resolved in preparation for planetary transmutation. There is no longer time enough, as there once was in the

60's and 70's, to repose leisurely while contemplating philosophically whether attention to the rumors of a new age is enlightened or worthwhile, for the transitions are already underway. All those who are able-bodied, who have a dedicated heart, and who possess a comprehending and resolute mind, should brace and ready themselves, for they are needed today to aid those of humanity who are less prepared.

Many people all over the world are most aware of the inevitable upheavals to come and are consequently effecting serious *material* measures in order to endure the impending tempest. However, relatively few such adaptive enthusiasts realize that it is the *inner cataclysm* with which they ought to be more concerned today. The greatest changes during the birth of the New World shall issue forth from the inner planes, and not from the external or physical plane, the results upon which shall be merely outward symptoms of far greater internal causes. Therefore, if it is to be known at all, the real turmoil will be experienced from within, and not from outer conditions.

As long as our objectives lie within the material plane we shall necessarily be wholly subject to the laws that pertain to the physical world. *Energy follows thought, and that which is focused upon grows.* If we work only in the material sense, we inevitably increase the load that crushes our own spirit. If we prepare in fear to save ourselves, we shall instigate new and deleterious causes in our self-regard which, under the now expedited Law of Karma, will only increase our struggle. It matters not where and how we are situated physically in the times ahead; much more dramatically will our well-being and prospects be affected by the *attitude* that we have fostered. Whether our outlook is of the old and selfish or of the new, expansive and life-enhancing, will significantly influence the deciding factors for our destiny at the Harvest Time. If our personal desires can be sublimated by right understanding we shall possess a great deal more ability to lift ourselves beyond the physical plane and its conditions. Indeed, if the subtle directives of the New Spirit are followed faithfully, then we shall be guided perfectly at the right time and from within to a most appropriate and optimum place for us in perfect accordance with our karma and merit. So now is the time to learn to trust life, to remain humble, to attune to our own intuitive guidance, and so go forth in helpfulness with regard for the good of the whole.

Of vital import today is the attainment of inner, divine-contact, and this will procure the freedom, strength and confidence that is born of true, spiritual vision. The bewilderment generated by false teachings and teachers, pseudo-visionaries and prophets, glamour, lower psychism, and all those superfluous props that tend to elicit distraction, attachment, confusion, scepticism, or even sheer disbelief regarding the real and vital truths and laws of the Aquarian age, will thus dissolve in the light of true seeing and unequivocal knowing. Similarly, when we abandon doubtful rationalization and subconscious reservation, and when we surrender to that which our hearts—not our heads—assure us is true, no matter what others think, then, and only then, can the Spirit work through us in perfect harmony for the benefit of all.

Humanity is and has always been responsible for the unfoldment of its destiny, and is faced today with an essential choice that must and will be made by everyone alike. The time for making the right decision and for appropriate action is *now*, for it takes time to integrate new understanding and new ways of being into our lives. Our choices today will profoundly affect our unforeseeable future, not just for this one present incarnation, but indefinitely, due to the gravity of the impending major Judgement Day. This so-called Judgement Day, however, should not be regarded with dread as a kind of doomsday decree upon mankind for its perpetrated evils of the past; to do so would be to subscribe foolishly to the antiquated and superstitious attitudes belonging to the minds of yesterday which knew no better. To the contrary, the preceding years leading up to the more appropriately-termed Harvest Time present a great blessing for humanity; an unprecedented opportunity to resolve past karma quickly, to release deleterious patterns of thought and emotion, to raise personal and planetary vibrations, and to help one another to emerge triumphant into the New World by *loving* through all the forthcoming changes. Success is assured for those who righteously persevere to the end.

With regard to this being the most important message in the world today, one might ask: is it not rather pompous, nay, blasphemous! to compare one's own vision more favorably than the great dispensations given by our spiritual masters, prophets and saints of the past? In order to answer this question fairly and appropriately, the following facts are now offered for due consideration by the earnest seeker.

The essential verities retained within past religious dispensations and spiritual traditions are, of course, most certainly as valid and valuable today with regard to the moral development of mankind as they were at the time of their introduction to the world.

However, with the exception of a small number of prophecies that were made very much in advance, the great teachers and spiritual leaders of the past were naturally less concerned with the very real and pressing exigencies that are evident in our present times; their guidance was simply not given for these remarkable days of both expanding spiritual opportunity and challenging adversity. While living amidst the escalating vibrations of negativity, worry, fear, etc., which are today infecting an ill-prepared humanity, old religious dogmas and ideals are becoming increasingly difficult to practice effectively in the way that their exponents may have conceived during a less intense period.

The current and imminent transformations, together with the new and adjusted laws of this Aquarian age under which they occur, have not been thoroughly addressed by the old creeds and faiths. Therefore, past religious or spiritual techniques may not be applicable today in the same way as they once were. Although some adherents of the old traditions and established codes of theology may be sincere, they perhaps fail to realize that tenets that were presented to and for the general awareness of mankind in centuries past will avail them little in gaining a good or even adequate understanding of the oncoming changes and the need of the present moment. The uniqueness and urgency of these times demands new teachings, new understanding and perception, timely response and appropriately righteous activity, and those who remain idealistically attached to the past presentations of spiritual truths and doctrines, and who endeavor, even though in earnest, to conduct their lives in accordance with the directives of scriptural or related texts alone, may fail to recognize and therefore benefit from the necessarily adjusted methods of present day spiritual guidance; guidance which is essentially concerned with preparation for Harvest: the most important opportunity in the world today.

In the words of Thoreau: *"How astonishing is this that of all the supreme revelations of truth, the world admits and tolerates only the more ancient, those which answer least to the needs of our epoch, while it holds each direct revelation, each original thought for null, and sometimes hates them."*

And: *"One should not think that a religion is true because it is old. On the contrary, the more mankind lives, the more the true Law of Life becomes clear to him. To suppose that in our epoch one must continue to believe what our grandfathers and ancestors believed is to think that an adult can continue to wear the garments of children."* — Tseng Tse.

Tolstoy expresses a similar sentiment: *"Let us not fear to reject from our religion all that is useless, material, tangible as well as all that is vague and indefinite; the more we purify its spiritual kernel, the more we shall understand the true Law of Life."*

And: *"For the letter killeth, but the Spirit giveth life."*—II Corinthians.

Times change, and so does consciousness. It is a most worthwhile and indeed necessary measure today to prepare our *vessels* so that they may be worthy to contain the *new wine* that is being poured most liberally upon everyone alike from the heavens (the inner dimensions of life). A full or closed vessel cannot receive any new wine, and the children of the New World therefore remain open and stand ready for the instant recognition of that which is new, relevant and true. They are eager for the immediate grasp of the truth of the times and they are treading the new way in the unfoldment of the pioneering human consciousness, while receiving the revelation—steadily and constantly presented by the emerging life—of the new and superseding paradigms that shall illuminate their path into the New World.

The attitude of all awakening individuals today, then, is set for the prompt relinquishing of all that is futile, unnecessary and inadequate to the need of the hour, and for the reception of that Power from on-high that necessarily breaks and destroys all that which has become crystallized, which has served its purpose fully, and which is consequently redundant. The man of the New World is therefore ready to work as a servant of the Divine Plan in accord with his true vision, reaching out compassionately in service to humanity.

Due to the rapidly expanding light of the New Spirit upon Earth today, perhaps it is not surprising that the seeds of a new religious dispensation are being sown in those minds that are fertile; a new religion[*] that will duly accommodate the New World Consciousness, the new and adjusted laws, and all the various

---

[*] The Latin word *Religare* means to *re-link* or *reunite*. True religion offers a dependable system for purification and re-alignment with the divine Spirit. It lucidly and unequivocally presents the truth of universal law and, unlike most of the existing religious dispensations, is not formulated or utilized to control people. Therefore, the new religion should not be compared to those extant today which are actually but shades of their pure and original form.

modern conditions that shall manifest in the Aquarian age. Regarding life and events in the light of spiritual values will facilitate the dissemination of the new teachings to mankind, and these will provide the blueprint of the new religion, thus offering humanity a fresh and truer understanding of the Divine Plan, and new insight into the great minds of those who implement it upon Earth, and who are the engineers of humanity's future.

The best of the virtues and advantages of the past religions will be brought forward into the New World and updated, taking due consideration of the new realities. The new religion will be a *world religion*. With the dawning of unity consciousness as well as greater intelligence and awareness generally upon the planet, no longer will mankind be so disposed to segregate itself by multifarious and complex presentations of the One Universal Truth as has been the case in the past, and to great disadvantage worldwide. Free of dogma and distinguished not by doctrines, the New World Religion will not be exemplified by theological psychologies or through organized sectarian groups and churches, but by an earnestly-loving inner attitude and natural orientation towards the truly spiritual life. The tenets of the new way will be scientifically-based, i.e., they will elicit greater practical insight into the Ageless Wisdom and will re-present esoteric principles that shall be proven by application and subsequent experience. As true, heart-inspired religious ceremonies and prayers take place at the same hour with common understanding and with identical spiritual intent all around the globe, the powerful, collective invocation of the united family of humanity will penetrate far deeper into the hidden worlds, and more than ever before will consequently evoke a correspondingly profound response from divine spheres. In demanding attention and succor from the higher planes, such forceful and vertical appeal will assure the reinstatement and preservation of "Heaven on Earth," and this new way will emerge fully when humanity is ready to really live its teachings.

The New World Religion will largely contribute toward the re-emergence upon Earth of what have been known in the past as *Mystery Schools*, together with their public acclaim, support and respect, although in the future there will be far fewer mysteries and secrets withheld from humanity than has, due to ignorance, necessarily been the case heretofore.

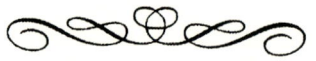

The Call to Action

THERE IS AN OLD FABLE THAT TELLS OF the events surrounding a certain Mother Hen who lived on a farm . . .

Now, Mother Hen wished to bake a cake for all the farm animals to enjoy, and being rather an astute and equitable fowl, she decided to appeal for some help in its preparation.

So she first approached Ermitrude the cow with her invitation to help, but, somewhat irritated, Ermitrude replied, "Moo! Can you not see that I am presently engaged in chomping this wonderfully lush green grass, garnished with daisies? I could not possibly risk forsaking this happy opportunity to dine just to help you make a cake."

Undaunted, Mother Hen soon afterwards espied Ferdinand the fox, eying her surreptitiously from behind a tree. She decided that discretion might be the better part of valor, and greeted him courteously yet vigilantly with her most reasonable request. Ferdinand responded in a rather contemplative and cool manner, "Hmmm," he mused. "If I help you to make a cake, then I shall have much less time to hunt for my vixen and cubs; a very demanding responsibility, of course, and one that requires much forward planning, careful rumination and adequate reflection. No, I need all my time, Mother Hen, and care not to waste any of it in pursuing mere trifles. However, there was something else I wanted to speak with you about . . . !"

Somewhat discomposed, Mother Hen ventured hastily forth from her rather apprehensive encounter with Ferdinand the fox, and presently encountered Derek, the farm's guard-dog, basking in the sun. "Hello Derek!" she clucked. "Will you help me make a cake for us all to eat for dinner tonight?"

Derek lazily managed to lift one eyelid, growled in lethargic disapproval at being disturbed, and proceeded to shift himself into a more comfortable position where he resumed his restful duty . . . .

The fable continues similarly and at length (as most fables are wont to do) as Mother Hen continues upon her righteous quest around the farmyard, attempting diligently to muster some assistance in order to make her cake. She meets with like excuses and unhelpful responses from Selena the sow, Herbert the horse and indeed all the other farmyard animals whom she politely entreats, including the inhabitants of her very own chicken coop, who all seemed far more interested in pecking at the ground than in baking a cake.

Rather flustered and in less than fine feather, Mother Hen is circumstantially compelled to toil alone for the rest of that day. However, the *prize for her tenacious labors is splendid indeed, and a great big mouth-watering cake is born by dinner time at six o' clock.*

Now, Mother Hen was certainly not a resentful or spiteful bird in any way, but she felt that it was her duty to teach the farm animals an important lesson. So she triumphantly took up the freshly baked, aromatic cake and wandered around the farmyard trumpeting proudly about her great achievement, and asking of everyone, "Now, who will help me eat this wonderfully tasty cake that I have baked all alone?"

With the greatest zeal, ALL the animals in the farmyard volunteered to assist Mother Hen in this most appealing task, but with a curt flutter of her wings, a dismissing wave of her rear feathers, and evincing a rehearsed air of indignation, she raked the ground beneath her feet and casually retorted, "I sounded the call, but no one came forth. Thus, since none of you have offered to help me create this most appetizing delicacy, then none of you are eligible to help me eat it either!"

Mother Hen proceeded that fair evening to enjoy a great feast, together with all her chicks.

✳ ✳ ✳

The searchlights of the many divine Agents who are assisting in the world-transformation are today sweeping the planet, singling out men and women who indicate spiritual potential and who bear a genuine love of humanity, of truth and of righteousness in their hearts. Their Call is being sounded worldwide from the inner side of life in order to rouse those who recognize something of the Divine Plan for mankind. It summons to activity all who are ready to gather together in order to realize the tremendous opportunities available at this time, and to share them openly for the good of all.

Servers in spirit have during the past decades been progressively stepping up the urgency of their all-important message. In the relatively recent past numerous channeled messages and telepathically-transmitted volumes have spoken to humanity from the hidden worlds. Now, specially designated members of both the spiritual Hierarchy of Earth and those of other world systems are themselves incarnating amongst us with very definite physical-plane missions. Such are these climactic times upon the planet, times that necessarily call for the complete cooperation and selfless dedication of humanity.

Many people, however, casually browse through information such as you are now reading and afterwards smugly assert to themselves and others that they already know all about the global transition. Demonstrating an air of self-satisfaction and even established authority, they often proceed to make absolutely no change in their lives whatsoever, lives that may be selfish and which are in these times, therefore, very precarious. Though not really surprising, such responses are ever a cause of concern for the discerning onlooker, for it is well understood that in order for success to be known, each person must absolutely remain humble, open, selfless, sympathetic and amenable during the period preceding the Harvest Time.

> *Men hear my words and understand them not, and then the carnal self purloins the seed, and not a sign of spirit life appears. Others hear the words of life, and with a fiery zeal receive them all; they seem to comprehend the truth and promise well, but troubles come, discouragements arise, there is no depth of thought; their good intentions wither up and die. These are the seeds that fell on stony ground. Others hear the words of truth and seem to know their worth, but love of pleasure, reputation, wealth and fame fill all the soil; the seeds are nourished not and they are lost. But others hear the words of truth and comprehend them well; they sink down deep into their souls; they live the holy life and all the world is blessed.* —Jesus.

Only that which we really *know* for ourselves becomes inherent faculty. The statements of a teaching, no matter how profoundly wise that teaching may be, will remain as but mental concepts until they are *experientially* a part of our lives. There is a tremendous distinction between accepting and understanding a truth intellectually and really living that truth in one's life; there is a very marked difference between common religiosity and true spirituality. If a man believes that he already knows best, then his cup is full and he can learn nothing new. Yet there is, of course, very much indeed in the world today that is new, and which is most worthy of an attentive and unassuming ear. Convictions are often a greater enemy of the truth than are lies. The ego always likes to think that it knows best and need not change or do anything special, and is most disposed to liberally broadcast its error, thereby spreading falsehood and confusion abroad by its wrong conviction. The rapidly approaching planetary deadline demands that such ignorant attitudes be transformed if successful emergence into the New World is to ensue.

The typical and clearly partially-informed attitude of the average so-called New Age person today affirms complacently the narrow belief that nothing special need be done, and that all grace will be bestowed in good time upon everyone alike without the need to make any effort whatsoever. This idea is absolutely untrue. Spiritual growth upon Earth progresses only in accord with the Law of Free Will. In passively allowing ourselves to be moulded by our surroundings, we ordinarily become, more or less, a product of our environment. Unless and until we make a conscious effort to rise above the norm, we shall inevitably remain programmed and limited by the established standards of our society. Such efforts may be observed in many adolescents as the soul attempts to motivate the developing personality to seek something higher than the extreme spiritual inertia that is demonstrated by the mass-consciousness. These natural impulses to transcend the mediocrity of modern society are most often considered as 'normal teenage rebellious behavior,' and are, therefore, treated accordingly. The ensuing suppression or condemnation from 'superiors' usually results in eventual conformity for the individual concerned and consequently a spiritually dull and unremarkable life. However, at this vital juncture in human development, should we remain inert, making no decisions, eliciting no action of our own volition and, therefore, allowing our will to abide in dormancy, then the Law of Recompense will remain at best neutral for us, and consequently nothing spiritually positive is going to come our way. Indeed, considering the general level of selfishness and negativity that abounds in the world today, as well as its infectious nature, just the opposite is likely to ensue. The sober individual may wish to seriously contemplate just how it may feel at the time of the Great Shift to experience a tremendous torrent of high-frequency energy as it surges through an unprepared personality who is host to numerous psychological and emotional impurities. This likelihood is today looming upon mankind's horizon, and is closer than most of us might like to believe.

If we do not awaken to the requirements that demand our attention and warranted discriminating activity today, then more severe measures will be appropriated for us by natural law. If we fail to demonstrate a timely and pertinent response to the intensifying hints in our lives, then let us not cry with surprise when eventually sledgehammers begin to fall! Just one seriously inappropriate choice in these times of acceleration and crisis may initiate karmic ramifications that could permanently close the door of opportunity. In addition, one day of selfishness may create the need for a great many more days of karmic redemption during the ever-decreasing time leading up to Judgement Day.

Adequate warning has been given to every soul repeatedly over numerous incarnations: *"Prepare ye! O prepare! for the Kingdom is at hand,"* yet still today humanity typically chooses pain as its teacher instead of love. Perhaps many will not believe the truth of the times until their familiar, comfortable but redundant reality begins to collapse all about them. Mostly, mankind will be forced to learn hard but necessary lessons during the coming upheavals, while those who see and understand will bide their time with discernment in usefulness as they await the Harvest Time in knowing anticipation. The years that lie immediately ahead may appear awful and devastating to secular vision, yet seen by the eyes of the divinely-aligned soul they will be recognized to be pregnant with the power of justice and righteousness. The urgently needed cleansing of the whole planet will include a torrential inrush of divine Light that will overwhelm and blind those who are unprepared, but will fill those who are ready with unsurpassed elation as they rejoice at the unveiled Truth. The one great enemy of Truth is self. Therefore, peril, regret, fear and dread lie ahead only for those who harbor the evil of selfishness, for mirrors line the way.

All those souls—whether incarnate or discarnate—who are residing upon the physical plane or within the subtle densities that interpenetrate and surround planet Earth, and who are responsible for creating disharmony, injustice, etc. in this, their current or previous incarnations, will presently be redressed, not by mankind's judgement, but by the strong and just hand of karmic law. It is especially imperative at this time to understand why we should never fight evil, for such violence only compounds our own problem. Rebellious thoughts of any kind harm the thinker and dissipate the power to overcome iniquity by righteousness. All aggressive reactions must be stayed, for in such reaction the truth of any situation can no longer be seen, and the aggressor becomes blinded to reality. As dispassionate witnesses, let the wise be an example to all in these "testing times" as they observe the unfolding of the Destiny of Ages. As we procure the life-raft of contemporary understanding, may we remain afloat during the coming tidal-floods of planetary cleansing by nurturing harmlessness and goodwill for the family of humanity.

※ ※ ※

The present *waiting period* preceding the time of the Great Shift provides a perfect opportunity for all those individuals with potential for harvest to prepare themselves by seeking, learning and, therefore, unfolding spiritually at a very quick pace. Such expeditious growth is possible due to the Aquarian energies that are flooding the planet, and also courtesy of the unprecedented assistance waiting to be given by divine Agents to all those who sincerely ask and who abide in selfless service. However, when the waiting period is over and the planetary deadline has arrived, events will appear to be moving so rapidly for most people that those who have not prepared themselves sufficiently will find that amidst the confusion and pandemonium they have no possibility to reflect upon and so rectify their failure to act expediently in good time.

Now is the time to prepare, and to prepare intelligently. This means more than merely reading a few New Age books and becoming self-satisfied in the erroneous idea that all good things will arrive in our laps effortlessly, and that we only need to wait and pray! The most critical advice in the world is today being trumpeted in all open ears by every single angel who is concerned with, and in attendance to, the greatest step ever taken by mankind on Earth: *"Humanity, with all your getting, get understanding."*

The new call to world salvage has gone out, and many people today are beginning to respond in various ways. Motives are usually mixed and response is frequently inspired by a desire for personal progress, recognition, aggrandizement, etc. Such reactions are at this particular time greatly complicating the call to action, and they are bringing about the fulfilment of the New Testament prophecy that at the time of the end there will be much distortion of the truth concerning the spread of the *Christ-Consciousness*, which shall be the crowning glory of the Great Transition.

The responsibility for appropriate action and effort to reach others with important and contemporary information rests upon the shoulders of those who see and who therefore understand. Dedicated assistance from mankind is a prerequisite if planetary upheavals are to be attenuated. The Earth's spiritual Elders are today inviting humanity to emerge from the wilderness of its selfish inertia for the sake of a world in need of healing. It is our *time* for which the great spiritual Hierarchies are today calling, it is our practical *activity* and *skill* that are required to aid all those who can be assisted, it is our *charity* and *love* which are so vitally needed, not only as a balm for the wounds of mankind, but also, and more importantly, for the dissemination of required and contemporary spiritual education and truly helpful guidance. It is our *service* that is demanded by prevailing conditions in order to facilitate contact with all those who are interested in joining together to contribute toward that which must be achieved. It is our *selfless meditation, inspiration,* inner and outer *devotion* and *invocation* that shall construct the channel through which the New Spirit may enter the physical plane. Great pain and suffering may be avoided in the immediate future by the acquisition of a true understanding of today's climactic circumstances, and the consequent application of that understanding in daily life.

The day of opportunity is with us, but it has its term. Today's unprecedented occasion, full of grace, is not forever lasting and will not dawn again for all those rejected souls for many thousands of years. The goals and purposes of the Divine Plan for this closing period of the Piscean age will come to an ultimate conclusion, and soon. The planetary time-clock will presently strike the hour, sounding the end of this cycle. At that moment those who are ready to receive the descent of higher frequencies will rise and prevail as they experience a victory of ages, and as the Earth passes into the glory of a more beautiful and expansive expression.

> *The wicked of the Earth will weep when they shall see the son of God come down upon the clouds of heaven, in power. Take heed you, O take heed, for you know not the hour nor the day when comes the son of God. Let not your hearts be overcharged with sensuous things, nor with the cares of life, lest that day come and find you unprepared. Keep watch at every season of the year; and pray that you may meet the Lord with joy and not with grief.* —Jesus

The Divine Plan for Earth cannot fail, for it is in perfect accord with the Great Scheme of Evolution designed by the Universal Architect; therefore it must and will go ahead. The new age will bring in a civilization, culture and fresh spirituality that shall be utterly different to anything hitherto known. All those of humanity who aspire to take their rightful place before the presently widening portal of opportunity that leads into the magnificence of the New World should ensure today that they are aware, dedicated, actively useful and so prepared.

Opportunity has been given by the invisible Servants of the race upon the inner side of life, and they now await humanity's active and positive response to their Call. They are watching lovingly, patiently and enthusiastically, and remain ever attentive to and supportive of all sincere efforts made toward aiding in the unfoldment of the Divine Plan, in the anchoring of the new energies upon Earth, and in the expeditious preparation for the imminent birth of the New World. These Great Beings are today poised above the planet, as it were, ready to activate the further inpouring of love, wisdom, light and healing force for the good of mankind. Receptivity is dependent upon a righteous and selfless attitude, and the prompt, positive and altruistic action of those who are aware and ready.

* * *

This is not merely just another book of exciting New Age information...

THIS IS YOUR CALL TO ACTION!

It is a most pertinent truism for today, more than ever before, that *"many are called, but few are chosen."* This is so due to a pervasive absence worldwide of a true appreciation of the gravity and opportunity of the times. Most people hear the call on some level—just as you are now—but they remain unchosen simply because they fail to respond positively to that call; they therefore exclude themselves from the promised glory.

When the false securities of the world that people have habitually cleaved to for so long begin to crumble around them, they shall not have the time nor the relaxed disposition to learn and integrate into their lives the timely lessons and principles expounded herein.

Now is your chance to make an intelligent and critical decision of your own volition, and before impending circumstances render that choice impossible for you.

Now is the perfect moment to embark uncompromisingly upon the path of understanding, and so prepare adequately for that which lies ahead.

Your immediate choices will shape the destiny of your own soul, and that of the world. Remember, everything is connected, and everyone is needed and has a role to play. Upon the great voyage into the new world there are no passengers; everyone is crew!

The New Call stresses emphatically its invitation for appropriate action. The greater message is: seek, get understanding, assemble, purify, prepare together, and invest yourself fully, without compromise, in some form of service to the world.

You now hold the map to spiritual success in your hands, but remember: the map is not the territory.

The Final Liberation

TODAY, AS WE ON EARTH ABIDE,
Evil compels us to take a side,
For it's a tool used to test our souls,
And should we fail, over us it controls.

So we need hear the message, and hear it right,
For evil is unleashed today with all its might,
And all those souls who did in past evil sow,
Will now feel that darkness within them grow.

These tempting forces of the shadow within,
Seek to bend our minds and make us sin,
And amidst such transgressions that are so unwise,
We may fall down far as all hear our cries.

As our sin seeks to clear from lifetimes past,
Our perception may brighten if the light we can grasp.
Yet should we react to such rising dark,
Then again evil is sure to make its mark.

So let us pay attention and listen hard,
For the time has come when we may get charred,
Just like a coal as it burns in the fire,
For all debts must be paid before we retire.

So, brothers and sisters, now we shall reap,
During the day and even as we sleep,
For evil powers and forces below,
Are arising fast as challenge they sow.

Such icy darkness so far from the Light,
Is being purged from the Earth and is seeking a fight.
All hatred, vengeance and cunning now free,
Will surely seduce all those who can't see.

As evil effects do draw to us near,
With right understanding we shall not fear,
For we are only reaping what we have sowed,
Let us then calmly accept lest we add to our load.

All negative reactions must be laid to rest,
For if they are not then we prolong our test.
Should we fail to embrace karma as forward we go,
Then we'll err again and pain we shall know.

Yet should we but see opportunity today,
Then occasion may be seized and grief kept at bay.
If we bend our will to do what is right,
We shall keep pending glory within our sight.

Our loving God from way up on-high,
Says, "Now is the time to do or to die.
Yes, souls do live forever and that you well know,
But those who fail now choose long delay below.

"Oh, dear, sweet children from out of My past,
Will you not see the light and do My Will at last?
Or will you forever on this Earthly plane roam,
Back and forth within the twilight zone?

"Oh, what silly children you all have been,
Living for self thinking you cannot be seen,
But now dear ones the truth will be known,
So prepare you all for your past to be shown.

"Be strong of heart and bold in faith,
Though mistakes have been made you've not yet lost the race,
For My great compassion from high above,
Will cleanse all those souls who now choose to LOVE."

So now is the 'testing time' spoken of old,
Time to do good or be left in the cold.
Our minds in this season will need to be,
In perfect control of all negativity.

And when our dark feelings begin to rise,
Deafening our ears and clouding our eyes,
We must remain calm with hands by our side,
For only thus can we the storm outride.

So we should be restrained as along we go,
Doing no wrong lest we know more woe,
Let us keep a tight rein upon mouth and mind,
And by living in truth, to others be kind.

But should we proceed to think selfishly,
In breaking the Law we'll pay a large fee.
We must give of what we have, all that we own,
For if we cannot then grief will be known.

A penny in the pocket and we'll never go;
A camel through a needle's eye we cannot sew.
That which we cherish we may fight to retain,
And what we hold onto will become our bane.

Let us give as we can and serve as we may,
Reaching out to all who may come our way.
Compassion and forgiveness must be to the fore,
In dealing with all who come to our door.

So today the time, just like before,
Has come 'round for us to tend to the poor;

The needy and hungry must all be fed,
A pillow found and a comfortable bed.

Clothing too and medical supplies,
All these things will help ease their cries.
Shelters and havens must be prepared;
Family homes; all must be shared.

Many arrangements should be made in good time,
To put food in storage, to stow all the wine,
Nuts and seeds and rice and bread,
All this will be needed for those who have fled.

Mountains of food, tinned for sure,
Must be carefully placed under many a floor.
Money, you see, will all soon disappear,
As greed and suspicion erupts in mass fear.

So all must be sold and our bindings cut free,
While provisions are made for shortages to be,
For time is so precious, we have little left;
Soon, very soon, millions bereft.

And all of the servers and helping hands,
Must be pre-warned of the coming bands;
Groups of brigands rising tall,
Filled with madness and grasping all.

But those vengeful and violent who are suffering thus,
Are the ones who'll most need to rely on us,
For as their inner darkness rises to clear,
They, too, will emerge as angels dear.

So we must reach out and do what is right,
To help all of those in the coming plight;
To feed, clothe and shelter each person in need,
And thus in our charity *we* shall be freed.

It's crucial today that we all understand,
That the fate of our soul rests in our own hand;
If we cannot contain rising feelings within,
We may further fall dragging all of our kin.

Whatever we've caused along Life's Great Road,
Will now begin to surface, whatever the load;
We must all accept what happens to us,
With such understanding we'll avoid much fuss.

For 'tis a mighty test that we all now face,
Yet a chance to move on from this self-seeking race,
For greener pastures and joy evermore,
As angels guide us to Heaven's door.

Yet dark forces will try to fill us with doubt,
For misery loves company and they won't leave us out;
For eons have they toiled upon Earth in the dark,
They are thus well-practiced and cunning is their mark.

Indeed, in the darkness our souls *can* learn,
Yet age after age we shall wait our turn,
For trials must be passed and victory known,
Before at last we can soar all the way Home.

Harder and harder will life now get,
As more and more souls inwardly fret,
As tighter and tighter our nerves are reeled,
And hearts will be tested as emotions are steeled.

We must not falter but just look ahead,
Though many may suffer and fall down dead,
For every soul its own journey must take,
And each one of us our own choices must make.

Now, most people believe only what they are taught,
And such blind faith can with danger be fraught,
For religion and Truth are far, far apart,
Thus the Aquarian age gives all a fresh start.

A new presentation to all who on Earth stroll,
Which seeks to draw out a response from the soul,
Of any true heart under the sun,
No matter what in past they may have done.

And thus in this prophesied 'time of the end,'
Is given one last chance for our ways to amend;
Great opportunity to come in from the cold,
The Final Liberation that was promised of old.

But many have been taught: 'Jesus will us save,'
Yet these words of untruth are born of the knave;
Jesus came only to *show* us the way,
Now it's our turn to *act* just as he in his day.

It is clear to some that these words are not new,
Yet the one who can see knows them to be true,
For each man saves himself, of this let's be sure,
And only by LOVING, no less and no more.

We must make the effort now to be true,
As we walk this last short road into the New.
Liberation is sure for each and every one,
Who acts as a conduit for the spiritual Sun.

So let us make haste to see this truth,
And in service to all let none stand aloof.

It is we who choose just where we shall go,
Our level of love and joy lets us know.
Let us open our hearts as never before,
And release our past karma by loving much more,
For only when clear will we truly be,
Prepared to fly Home for all to see.

Today the reaping bins do overflow,
From evil sown millions of years ago;
Deeds done in past by resolute men,
Who played with fire but can't recall when.

Now as we behold the fulfilment of Law,
We shall all recollect what we did before;
When old memories resurrect for us to see,
We shall understand well that justice must be.

Yet 'tis not our task to vengeful be,
For the universe brings balance naturally,
So we seasoned wanderers from out of the past,
Must do our best to spread this truth fast.

Truth and foreknowledge of that which shall be,
Carries the power to set each man free,
For right understanding surely guides our way,
As it directs our thoughts and actions each day.

So may the sweetness of Truth help us to see,
May we be blessed daily with new clarity,
Thus we shall emerge from out of life's maze,
Our thoughts fully cleansed and all evil erased.

Calmer now and wiser for sure,
As we perceive the glory of that far distant shore;
All darkness is gone and our conscience is clear,
At last! At last! to our Home we draw near.

Maxims for the Aquarian Age

(reminders from the text)

- EVERY PERSON IS TODAY BEING COMPELLED to make a choice that shall greatly affect both the present course of their life and their future soul-development, throughout incalculable incarnations.

- Like a rainstorm, one of the chief and concluding effects of the impending tempest will be that of global purification.

- The impending and necessary cleansing of the Earth and of all sentient life thereupon may be difficult or moderate for each individual depending upon the degree of preparation attained.

- Denial or disregard of impending planetary developments will certainly not diminish them or prevent them from occurring.

- It is new understanding that will transform the world, not merely the desire for change.

- Those men and women who have embodied altruistic attitudes for much or all of their lives will be greatly advantaged in the times to come, as they are stimulated and exceptionally blessed by the incoming streams of new energy.

- For those who are virtuous and who have prepared themselves due to their understanding of the present world-crisis and opportunity, cosmic frequencies are and will continue to be responsible for many positive spiritual awakenings.

- As frequencies rise, the power of thought is magnified, affecting all of life much more tangibly and swiftly than heretofore.

- Each individual's consciousness (which is an integral part of the planetary vibration) must be raised to a minimal level in order to qualify for entrance into the New World.

- The easiest way to raise the vibration of consciousness for most people is to evoke the powers of the Spirit, and this may be done by focusing out of and away from the personal self, and upon some higher and worthy purpose.

- It is the demonstration of love alone that shall positively affect a person's consciousness and raise one's vibration.

- Today, at the end of this 75,000-year major cycle, and consequently due to the unprecedented grace afforded each and every person on Earth, it is much easier for all humanity to ascend in consciousness.

- The Aquarian age is not a time of workshops, courses and lectures; it is an era of active participation for the greater good.

- Active and altruistic response to the present need is demanded today in order for success to be known, not passive acquiescence.

- It is critical in these times to subscribe sincerely and fully to all that is new and righteous, for the Harvest Time is at hand.

- Generally, the greatest good that anyone can confer at this time upon Earth—for others as well as for themselves—is to help toward raising the planetary vibration, and this may be achieved by truly benevolent thinking and selfless, loving activity.

- Separation, on any level, is destructive; a relic of ignorance from the past.

- Cooperation and unity are the goals of the immediate future.

- Active goodwill is seen as the touchstone that will transform the world.

- Selfish spirituality is imitation spirituality.

- The forces of the old do not have the power to affect anyone who attunes to the New.

- The old cannot withstand the New, for such is the Divine Plan for humanity.

- Whoever is in conflict with anything through resistance, worry, fear, aversion, dependence or selfish desire of it is automatically of the old to the same degree as that conflict.

- It is by constructive and benign thinking alone that we may heal ourselves by rising above the dense and debilitating thought-clouds that we have unwittingly cultivated during an inimical past.

- If the mind makes a practice of rectitude in its thinking, there is no evil that can make entrance into it.

- The vibration of Love is both the greatest protector *and* benefactor in the universe.

- Positive thoughts and healthy emotions react most favorably upon both the subtle and physical bodies of man, and improve their ability to assimilate life-force and to receive other beneficial energies.

- Our inner biological pharmacopoeia is triggered in accordance with the unique events passed through and the subsequent choices made.

- All energies that have in past been successfully drawn upon by aspirants seeking self-improvement are today being withdrawn as the whole planet enters its next and higher level of expression.

- Today a new note is sounding forth: the note of growth through the service of the race.

- Spiritual aspirants are most truly progressing when they assist the progress of others.

- Under the laws of the Aquarian age, assistance is given only to those who have transcended selfish aspiration and lost sight of their own progress in the genuine and selfless impulse to be of service to others.

- Depending upon the purity of each individual's motives and orientation toward helpfulness rests the possibility of utilizing today's spiritual opportunities successfully.

- Success and survival during the birth of the New World is a question of *US*, not I.

- People need one another, and as soon as just a small increase in the percentage of the human race begins to truly appreciate the untold advantages of working together for a selfless cause, then, ensuing under the Law of Synergy, great accomplishments will be known—worldwide.

- Union is harmony and strength.

- Universal law guarantees that success will be known when a number of sincerely dedicated people work together with enthusiasm, perseverance and a common, unselfish focus.

- A period of time approaches when community and cooperative living will be essential to the survival of the race.

- No community will survive during and after the tribulations unless it is built and maintained upon the sure and sturdy foundations of a joint spiritual aspiration and a selfless ethic.

- True community resides in the hearts of its members as a spiritual attitude, and not as some external objective or even a common desire to attain it.

- Communities of the new era may consist only of true friends.

- It is Love which is the *new currency* of the Aquarian age.

- Unity consciousness is the new keynote being sounded abroad today, and is the hallmark of the person in the New World.

- Upon the understanding response to the collective needs of mankind will depend the rapidity with which each person will be able to achieve the next revelation and expansion of consciousness which is, for him, possible.

- The expansion and radiation today of the New World Consciousness is one very potent principle that can salvage mankind and evoke that New Spirit which can and will build the New World.

- The Portal of Initiation leading to the New World may only be traversed in group-formation; such is a law of the Aquarian age.

- If group-collaboration is absent, if the true team-spirit is not being demonstrated today, then there is not much that the divine Helpers of the race upon the inner side of life can do for humanity in these unique times.

- Due to the present influx of spiritual energy in our solar system, group-potential is unparalleled today.
- Each member of the human family must now choose between love and fear, wisdom and ignorance.
- In the very near future, one way or another, each individual will have made a necessary choice to affiliate with either the *Islands of Light* or the *caverns of darkness*; there will be no grey areas.
- The dawning light of the New Day is throwing shadows in all directions.
- It is only by shining a light into darkness that we are able to see clearly and so deal with the shadow side of life in a positive way.
- Blind and unintelligent submission to external authorities is inherently dangerous.
- Spiritual teachers and gurus are not utilized today in the same unthinking and deferential way as in past times.
- The real and qualified spiritual teachers in the Aquarian age will not gather disciples around themselves.
- Psychism is not a sanction for true, spiritual work.
- Psychic ability does not necessarily (or even usually) correspond to spiritual purity.
- channeling (mediumship) constitutes a definite distraction to real spiritual attainment.
- Due to the extant ignorance of mankind and the intensity of the period, channeling today is proving itself to be more often a curse than a gift.
- One basic truth is often used as a foundation for a whole pile of deception.

- Earnest and intelligent seeking is the essential first step toward revelation and spiritual success.

- The very act of seeking sets natural forces in motion that greet the seeker in order to impart certain 'secrets' which that individual may be ready to behold; Life responds as if to an invitation.

- Humble seeking is an integral and inseparable part of the New World Consciousness.

- In demanding the attention of the Spirit, loving service is the great nemesis of the ego, for it threatens its very existence.

- In serving the Spirit in all we shall find that our own highest needs are met by way of such service.

- The path of spiritual service is the most splendid, noble and holy way; it is the Royal Road for which all other disciplines are but preparatory.

- If there ever was one solution to absolutely every problem throughout mankind's history, all the way up to the present and on into Eternity, it must surely be... *serve, and keep serving; give, and never stop giving.*

- Generally, the most valuable service that may be rendered today in this unique period is to spread the vital truth of the times.

- When we cease in our seeking for ourselves alone, and when in knowing greater freedom from the burdens created by personal desire we are able to demonstrate compassion and goodwill to others, we open a channel for the Love of Spirit to flow through us.

- Service is love in action.

- Service may be said to be the most supreme meditation, for it is the one great and eternal Meditation that endures within the Heart of the Universe itself.

- All who would cross the threshold between the old and the New and emerge into the magnificence of the New World must possess a genuine love of others and, therefore, an attitude that naturally impels their wish to be of service.

- The divine Helpers of the race can do little more for men than they would do for other men.

- Upon selflessly and appropriately sharing with others that which has been revealed to us, more is given from within.

- In the times ahead, all that which is held to oneself, anything that is not offered selflessly in service to others, and everything which is not contributed toward the One Divine Work upon Earth will be taken away.

- If it is to be known at all, the real turmoil during the coming times will be experienced from within, and not from outer conditions.

- As long as our objectives lie within the material plane, we shall necessarily be wholly subject to the laws which pertain to the physical world.

- If our personal desires can be sublimated by right understanding, we shall possess a great deal more ability to lift ourselves beyond the physical plane and its conditions.

- All those of humanity who aspire to take their rightful place before the presently widening portal of spiritual opportunity that leads into the magnificence of the New World, should ensure today that they are aware, dedicated, actively useful and so prepared.

- Opportunity has been given by those invisible Servants of the race upon the inner side of life, and they now await humanity's active and positive response to their call.

An ongoing Web forum presently exists to discuss the topics revealed in our first two books. Other writings that expand upon and complement the books are also available to subscribers. To apply for subscription to the Gateway forum, send a request to:

The-Gateway-subscribe@yahoogroups.com

Recommended Reading

The volumes listed below are highly recommended for today's studious seeker. Those titles that address this important time of the Earth's transition, the new and adjusted laws and teachings, etc., are marked by an asterisk (*).

A sound occult understanding will also be of invaluable assistance to the aspirant who plans to consciously enter the New World and to help others do the same. Therefore, unmarked book titles have also been included in the list. In addition to covering adequately the human microcosm—the inner constitution of man—these volumes offer most relevant and useful instruction about those unchanging principles, laws and verities that guide and govern all the spheres within this octave of the universe.

A Gift from Daniel—Karen Alexander
Awakening to Zero Point—Gregg Braden (*Chapters 1,5,6 & 7*) *
Astral Body, The—A E Powell
Brotherhood—Devorss Publications, CA. USA *
Causal Body, The—A E Powell
Celestine Prophecy, The—James Redfield *
From Bethlehem to Calvary—Alice Bailey
Hathor Material, The—Tom Kenyon & Virginia Essene *
Hidden Side of Things, The—C W Leadbeater
Light Emerging—Barbara A Brennan
Masters and the Path, The—C W Leadbeater
Mental Body, The—A E Powell
New Teachings for an Awakening Humanity—Virginia Essene *
Only Planet of Choice, The—Phyllis Schlemmer (*Chapters 1,7,8*) *
Phoenix Rising—Mary Summer Rain *
Revelation, The—Barbara Marx Hubbard *
Spiritual Philosophy for the New World, A—John Randolph Price *
Starseed Transmissions, The—Ken Carey *
Tenth Insight, The—James Redfield *
Third Millennium, The—Ken Carey *
Vision—Ken Carey *

Introducing

Servers of the Divine Plan

The Destiny of Ages is Nigh

DUE TO THE UNPRECEDENTED spiritual activity that is presently unfolding upon the planet, our globe has consequently become a busy nucleus of activity for interested parties originating from other planets, galaxies and dimensions. Members of various interstellar confederations have moved closer to Earth in order to assist with the now imminent Great Transition which shall positively affect all life on our world.

The memories and higher faculties of certain individuals are just today returning to them, and they are beginning to recall the purpose of their incarnation, their duty to humanity and to planet Earth. They are becoming aware of the close attendance of legions of incorporeal divine Emissaries, the exalted ranks to which they inherently belong. They are remembering that they are an essential part of a vast collective effort and tremendously important task, the scope of which stretches back across millions of years and a myriad of past lifetimes upon Earth and elsewhere, all geared toward the forthcoming and conclusive glory. In their remembrance, they are perceiving that they are about to realize the grand consummation of a vital phase of the Divine Plan for Earth, the solar system and beyond.

The Servers are awakening, and they are taking up their positions as agents of the New Spirit in order to play an active role within today's expanding world-consciousness around the planet.

> *This book not only unveils revelatory facts regarding the long-prophesied and now unfolding Aquarian Passion Play on Earth, but is also a very practical and instructive guide for those millions of individuals who are today awakening all over the world in line with the ongoing global transformations.*

Softback book may be purchased at
www.thenewcall.org

Or available free for download at
www.thenewcall.org/book_download.htm

Inner Teachings

WHEREVER WE LOOK TODAY within the spiritual supermarket there is restlessness, glamour and excitement, an eager pursuit for self-liberation, self-empowerment or 'ascension' from this world, the practice of low-grade psychism and an anxious fleeing from pain and responsibility—all in the name of spirituality.

As the long-prophesied influx of new light continues to enter our world, darkness is necessarily accentuated, and today the dawning light of the new Aquarian age is throwing shadows in all directions. The result? A great plethora of exaggeration, misinformation and imitation spirituality.

As stimulating psychic forces are being released and made available to mankind on an unprecedented scale, the unsuspecting, hasty and unenlightened are exhibiting their new abilities with remarkable alacrity, prematurely stepping forward to inaugurate themselves to the general public as spiritual teachers, healers and masters of wisdom.

These new teachers often offer fake spiritual gems that may appear to sparkle in the beginning, but soon fade and become lackluster, along with the temporary satisfaction which may have been initially gleaned from them, while simultaneously they serve only to lead aspirants further and further away from the simple Truth.

However, that Truth is ever present and accessible by those who know where to look, and so who are able to find the Golden Key that unlocks the door to New Life.

* * *

At the end of every world cycle, a fresh and unadulterated form of the *Universal Doctrine*—or *Gnosis*—makes its reappearance on Earth in order to call in from the fields, before the Harvest Time, all those who are able to understand and apply it in their lives, and so meet the requirements of the latest cyclic opportunity for spiritual Deliverance.

The much needed rekindling of the Perennial Wisdom-Teaching of the Avatars in times of spiritual darkness signifies an informed effort to replace the plethora of misinterpretations, distortions and falsifications that will have inevitably spread throughout the world's religions and spiritual traditions over the centuries. It is, therefore, an important part of a truly religious endeavor to reestablish the Truth in the world and to thus contribute toward sounding the Final Call to humanity at the end of an age prior to the necessary planetary cleansing.

The word *Gnosis* is derived from the Greek language and means *Knowledge of God*, or *Divine Knowledge*. The Gnosis itself is Living Wisdom, unobtainable through the use of the intellect alone. However, when the earnest seeker of Truth utilizes the mental faculty in the right way, for the right reasons and in combination with the heart, he may be brought into contact with the Living Body that is Gnosis by way of the printed letter of the Law.

Although the Universal Knowledge that is of the Gnosis constitutes the foundation of every true religion, it has been expunged or, at best, grossly distorted in all those religious traditions that still exist today.

Presently, very few people in the world possess the vital Key that is Pure Gnosis, and this is one of the reasons why there is so much confusion, distraction, futility and sham spirituality abroad at this frantic time on the planet. Yet this very same Key has been discovered and used by every great spiritual luminary throughout Earth's history. All of these enlightened individuals found the One True Path that leads directly to the summit of Life, and in embarking upon the Lighted Way, they managed to bypass the multitudinous enticements and snares in the world of delusion to arrive safely Home. Today, we seek to free genuine candidates for harvest from all superfluous hubbub by placing before them esoteric facts that are as old as the planet, yet which have been re-presented in a modern format, taking into consideration today's grand opportunity as well as the new and adjusted laws of the Aquarian age.

* * *

It has been stated in the Hatha Yoga Pradapika: *"It [yoga] gives liberation to Yogis and bondage to fools."* Similarly, and with regard to The Pure Gnosis, we would say that it may be liberating for earnest and mature seekers on the Path but onerous and thus potentially detrimental for less dedicated and, therefore, unprepared aspirants.

In times past, the Inner Teachings of the Universal Doctrine were given only to Initiates of genuine Mystery Schools, where stringent tests had to be passed before entrance to the Divine Mysteries was permitted. We are offering such information today to those who are ready because we are in the "end times."

Due to the revelatory and uncompromising esoteric nature of

that which is given in our advanced writings, they are reserved only for those serious and intelligent spiritual aspirants who know how to knock aright and so who already possess the key that unlocks the door.

> *Let him who seeks continue seeking until he finds. When he finds he will become troubled, and when he becomes troubled he will be astonished. . . .* —Jesus, *The Gnostic Gospel of Thomas.*

Printed in the United States
31162LVS00002B/679-759